# Global Retailing

# Global Retailing

 International Council of Shopping Centers

# About the International Council of Shopping Centers

The International Council of Shopping Centers (ICSC) is the trade association of the shopping center industry. Serving the shopping center industry since 1957, ICSC is a not-for-profit organization with more then 54,000 members in 96 countries worldwide.

ICSC members include shopping center

- owners
- developers
- managers
- marketing specialists
- leasing agents
- retailers
- researchers
- attorneys
- architects
- contractors
- consultants
- investors
- lenders and brokers
- academics
- public officials

ICSC holds more then 200 meetings a year throughout the world and provides a wide array of services and products for shopping center professionals, including publications and research data.

For more information about ICSC, please contact:
International Council of Shopping Centers
1221 Avenue of the Americas, 41st Floor
New York, NY 10020-1099
Telephone: (646) 728-3800
Fax: (732) 694-1755
http://www.icsc.org

Companies, professional groups, clubs and other organizations may qualify for special terms when ordering quantities of more than 20 of this title.

Published by
INTERNATIONAL COUNCIL OF SHOPPING CENTERS
Publications Department
1221 Avenue of the Americas
New York, NY 10020-1099

Book Design: Harish Patel Design
Cover Design: Design Plus

ICSC Catalog Number: 248

International Standard Book Number: 1-58268-064-7

# Contents

# Introduction

As the global economy continues to expand, retail and development opportunities abound. While developers are tapping into emerging markets and other areas of potential growth, retailers have been challenged to customize their retailing efforts to meet the demands of varying marketplaces and at the same time maintain a strong and recognizable brand. To compete effectively and efficiently, the best global retailers are taking advantage of advanced marketing and distribution vehicles to manage consumer demand.

In fact, according to Deloitte Touche Tohmatsu in a report entitled "2006 Global Powers of Retailing" published in *Stores* magazine, January 2006:

- *The predominant operations formats continue to be food-related. Nearly 60% of the top retailers sell food, with most operating a variety of formats including supermarkets, hypermarkets/supercenters, hard discount stores, cash & carry/warehouse clubs, and convenience stores.*

- *Over half of the top retailers operate specialty retailing concepts. In particular, retailers specializing in homegoods categories have flourished in a strong housing market, and a burgeoning middle class around the world boost demand for consumer electronics, home improvement products and services, and home furnishings.*

- *Multi-channel retailing continues to grow, with more retailers developing an e-commerce capability.*

In light of this new era of global opportunities, ICSC's *Global Retailing* was developed to enlighten and encourage shopping center professionals worldwide and consists of over 75 detailed retailer profiles that report pertinent sales and operations data, share successes, and feature color photographs throughout.

The retailers profiled in this publication are a sampling of retailers operating in multiple countries and were selected by an editorial team primarily based on retail sales and number of countries of operation. Retailers wishing to be included in future editions of *Global Retailing* may contact ICSC's Publications Department for consideration.

# Global Retailers

# AEON CO., LTD.

| | |
|---|---|
| **Parent Company/ Corporate Name:** | **AEON CO., LTD.** |
| Corporate Retail Headquarters: | 1-5-1 Nakase, Mihama-ku, Chiba-shi, Chiba 261-8515, Japan +81-43-212-6042 www.aeon.info |
| Annual Revenue: | $36.3 billion (2004) |
| Number of Locations: | 5,124 |
| Countries of Operation: | Japan, Hong Kong, Malaysia, China, Taiwan, the Philippines, South Korea, Thailand |
| Retail Classification: | Supermarket, convenience stores, hypermarket, drug. specialty |

*Aeon Co., Ltd., owns or franchises over 5,000 stores worldwide and offers food services in over 330 locations..*

AEON CO., LTD. owns or franchises over 5,000 stores worldwide. It is Japan's largest supermarket chain, with 1,050 stores known as Maxvalu. It also operates 2,300 Ministop convenience stores (famous for their soft ice cream) and 450 JUSCO superstores. Its EDLP ("everyday low price") concept is used throughout its general merchandise and grocery operations.

The company's history dates back to 1758, when Sozaemon Okada began trading in kimono fabrics and accessories. That "thread" continues today, as AEON operates a number of specialty chains, including Talbots, Blue Grass (apparel for teens and younger women), Cox (family casual apparel), Laura Ashley Japan, AEON Forest, Mega Sports (The Sports Authority in Japan), Claire's Nippon, Nustep and others. It owns a majority interest in the Talbots women's clothing chain. AEON has recently expanded into the drugstore business as well, with its 1,900-plus AEON Welcia stores, through which it is developing the "Happy Face" cosmetics brand name. Some of these stores find their way into AEON Mall Co., Ltd.'s shopping center development operation, which includes more than 14 complexes, and which expanded into property management in 2003.

AEON also offers food services in over 330 locations through its Gourmet d'Or and Jack stores. It also has 170-plus AEON Fantasy outlets — indoor amusement spaces populated by original characters who give live performances and interact with children.

Beyond Japan, AEON runs about 34 stores, including recent expansions into Malaysia, China and Taiwan.

*T*albots, Blue Grass, Cox and Mega Sports (The Sports Authority in Japan) are among their specialty chains.

# Aldi Group

| | |
|---|---|
| **Parent Company/ Corporate Name:** | **Aldi Einkauf GmbH & Co., oHG** |
| Corporate Retail Headquarters: | (Nord:) Eckenbergstr. 16 16 45307 Essen-Kray, Germany +49-0-201-8593-0 |
| | (Sud:) Burgstr. 37-39 45476 Mülheim a.d. Ruhr, Germany www.aldi.com |
| Annual Revenue: | $43 billion (2004) |
| Number of Locations: | 6,936 |
| Countries of Operation: | Australia, Austria, Belgium, Denmark, France, Germany, Ireland, Luxembourg, The Netherlands, Spain, the U.K., the U.S. |
| Retail Classification: | Supermarkets |

*A*ldi prides itself on the freshness of its produce. Stores also carry household supplies and health and beauty products.

Aldi Group is an international retailer specializing in a limited assortment of private-label, high-quality products. Two independent and autonomous companies comprise Aldi Group: Aldi Nord (north), based in Essen, and Aldi Süd (south), based in Mülheim. Each is run by one of the brothers who took over the grocery business from their father in the early 1960s. Foreign activities are also clearly divided between the two companies. Price reductions are the only area in which the two companies work jointly.

Aldi is among the most-talked-about retailers in Europe, with many defenders and critics of its policies, particularly those related to employment and customer service. Self-service is the key. Cans and packages are stacked in boxes piled atop pallets. There may be only one or two brands of some products. But the prices are "delightfully, breathtaking low," according to *Business Week* magazine — so much so that superretailer Wal-Mart struggles against Aldi in Germany.

Aldi stores eliminate "costly extras that increase the price of the products you buy at other grocery stores." Grocery carts must be rented (for about 25 cents U.S.), and the rental fee is refunded when one returns the cart to the corral after loading the car with groceries. Customers are encouraged to recycle grocery bags by bringing used bags on subsequent shopping trips, but bags may be purchased for a nominal fee. Bagging clerks, check cashing and preferred customer savings cards are other extras foresworn by Aldi.

Aldi is known for efficiency and productivity, although its range of products is quite small for a supermarket: less than 1,000, and often only

about 650, which are almost all Aldi–exclusive labels. Only those articles that have proven themselves to be fast movers at test stores are taken throughout the chain. The company prides itself on the freshness of its produce and the quality of its canned fruits and vegetables. Stores also carry frozen food, meat and dairy, breads, household supplies, health and beauty products and cleaning products.

In the U.S., Aldi operates nearly 800 stores in 26 states. Besides Germany (3,900-plus stores), Aldi has a strong presence in France (576 stores), The Netherlands (388 stores), Belgium (375 stores), and other countries.

*B*esides 3,900-plus stores in Germany, Aldi has a strong presence in France, The Netherlands, Belgium and the U.S.

# Apple Store

**Apple Store** Worldwide

| | |
|---|---|
| **Parent Company/ Corporate Name:** | **Apple Computer, Inc.** |
| Corporate Retail | 1 Infinite Loop Cupertino, CA 9504, United States (408) 996-1010 www.apple.com |
| Annual Revenue: | $14 billion (2005) |
| Number of Locations: | 50 |
| Countries of Operation: | The U.S., the U.K., Canada, Japan |
| Retail Classification: | Electronics |

*An Apple Store is a good place to learn about Apple products, including the Macintosh computer.*

©Mark Milian

*Consumers can experience the complete line of Apple products, from computers to iPods, at an Apple Store.*

At an Apple Store, consumers can experience the complete line of Macintosh computers and an amazing array of digital cameras, camcorders, the entire iPod family and much more in a very inviting atmosphere.

The interactive Apple Store is a place to ask questions and get answers. And it's the best place to learn about the "Mac." There is plenty of staff on hand eager to help customers discover the "Mac" that's right for them.

Consumers can fully experience the digital lifestyle on a "Mac" at one of Apple's own retail stores. The "try-before-you-buy" approach continues to prove well for both the retailer and the consumer. There are currently over 120 stores in approximately 30 states across the United States and 13 stores within the U.K., Canada and Japan.

# Arcadia Group

| | |
|---|---|
| **Parent Company/ Corporate Name:** | **Taveta Investments** |
| Corporate Retail Headquarters: | Colegrave House, 70 Berners Street London W1T 3NL, United Kingdom +44-20-7636-8040 www.arcadiagroup.co.uk |
| Annual Revenue: | $3 billion (2004) |
| Number of Locations: | 2,000 |
| Countries of Operation: | Austria, Bosnia, Chile, Croatia, Cyprus, Denmark, Germany, Gibraltar, Iceland, Israel, Kuwait, Malaysia, Malta, Oman, the Philippines, Poland, Portugal, Qatar, Saudi Arabia, Singapore, Slovenia, Spain, Sweden, Turkey, the United Arab Emirates, the U.K. |
| Retail Classification: | Specialty |

Arcadia Group is the U.K.'s #1 apparel retailer, with 2,000 high-end stores, largely in urban areas. The company began with a single menswear store in 1900, quickly expanding to 10 and achieving further growth by supplying uniforms for one-fourth of Britain's armed forces in World War I.

The company expanded into women's apparel in 1946, and its women's chains now include Dorothy Perkins, Miss Selfridge, Wallis, Topshop and Evans. Its men's stores include Burton and Topman.

*A*rcadia Group's chains include Wallis, Miss Selfridge, Dorothy Perkins, Burton and Topman.

Arcadia Group also has several hundred franchised stores in about 30 countries in Europe, the Mideast, Asia and South America in a addition to its Dial Home Shopping service of catalog and Internet retailing businesses. Arcadia became part of Taveta Investments in 2002.

*In addition to its cata log and internet retailing businesses, the company has several hundred franchised stores located in Europe, the Mideast, Asia and South America.*

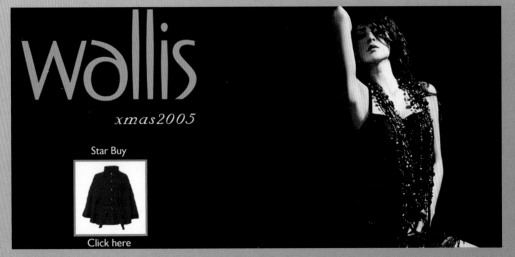

# Auchan Group

**Auchan**

| | |
|---|---|
| **Parent Company/ Corporate Name:** | **Auchan Group** |
| Corporate Retail Headquarters: | 200 rue de la Recherche 59650 Villeneuve d'Ascq Cedex, France +33-3-28-37-67-00 www.auchan.com |
| Annual Revenue: | $37.4 billion (2004) |
| Number of Locations: | 900 |
| Countries of Operation: | Argentina, China, France, Hungary, Italy, Luxembourg, Morocco, Poland, Portugal, Russia, Spain, Taiwan |
| Retail Classification: | Hypermarket, supermarket |

*With over 320 hyper-markets and more than 600 supermarkets in 12 countries, Auchan Group is among the world's largest retailers.*

With over 320 hypermarkets and more than 600 supermarkets in 12 countries, from Portugal to Taiwan, Auchan Group is among the world's largest retailers.

Accounting for more than 19% of the Group's sales, the supermarket division is found in five countries. Store renovations and trials of new services have marked recent activity. Discounting is being tried in its Italian Cityper stores. Acima, in Morocco, developed smaller formats to capitalize on the bulk-buying habits of customers. In its Italian Sma stores, Auchan tested a "self check-out" system. Spain's Sabeco stores told customers, "Saber comprar, saber economisar" ("Knowing how to buy is knowing how to save").

The hypermarket division served over 648 million customers in 12 countries in 2003, accounting for 78% of the Group's sales. These stores carry groceries, apparel, consumer electronics, travel services and fast food. The Group continues to open new stores in new locations. In all countries, the hypermarkets continue the low-price policy established in 2001 and place new importance on promotions and customer loyalty programs. Auchan is expanding its reliance on regional products and local agricultural supply lines.

The company opened its first outlet in Roubaix, France, in 1961. Auchan withdrew from the U.S. and Mexico markets in 2003. The Group also runs Leroy Merlin, one of France's premier home improvement retail chains.

*Groceries, apparel, consumer electronics and fast food can be found in their hypermarkets. Auchan also offers banking and travel services.*

# Benetton Group S.p.A.

**UNITED COLORS OF BENETTON.**

| | |
|---|---|
| **Parent Company/ Corporate Name:** | **Benetton Group S.p.A.** |
| Corporate Retail Headquarters: | Villa Minelli 31050 Ponzano Veneto Treviso, Italy 39-0422-519111 www.benetton.com |
| Annual Revenue: | € 1.7 billion (2004) |
| Number of Locations: | 5,000 |
| Countries of Operation: | 120 |
| Retail Classification: | Apparel |

*T*he United Colors of Benetton brand offers casual clothes known for their color, energy and practicality.

*B*rand lines include Playlife leisure wear, Killer Loop streetwear and the fashion-oriented Sisley.

*P*

Present in 5,000 stores worldwide, the Benetton Group produces about 110 million garments each year. While strongly influenced by the styles of its native Italy, its designs have achieved an international acceptance through its four main brands.

The United Colors of Benetton brand offers casual clothes known for their color, energy and practicality. The apparel line has an advertising presence that speaks to its universality. The brand is broadening its horizons, expanding into new areas such as kitchen accessories, terrycloth, baby products, toiletries, perfumes and watches. Undercolors is yet another expansion of the brand, with its own chain of 500 stores in 30 countries.

Rounding out the brand lines are Playlife leisurewear, Killer Loop streetwear and footwear, and the fashion-oriented Sisley brand, which accounts for about 20% of the firm's sales.

Founded in 1965, the first Benetton store in Paris opened four years later. By the 1990s, the chain had expanded to 120 countries. In the new millennium, Benetton's has followed the market patterns and opened a network of megastores,

which carry casual clothing and underwear for men, women and children, as well as a wide variety of accessories.

© Miguel Casanelles

*B*enetton is broadening its horizons by expanding into new areas such as home design and kitchen accessories.

© Vangelis Paterakis

# The Body Shop

TM ©Vismedia

| Parent Company/<br>Corporate Name: | **The Body Shop International plc** |
|---|---|
| Corporate Retail<br>Headquarters: | Watersmead, Littlehampton<br>West Sussex BN17 6LS, United Kingdom<br>+44-1903-731-500<br>www.the-body-shop.com |
| Annual Revenue: | £419 million (2005) |
| Number of Locations: | 2,045 |
| Countries of Operation: | 52 within North America, Europe, Asia, Africa, Australia. |
| Retail Classification: | Skin and body care |

©Vismedia

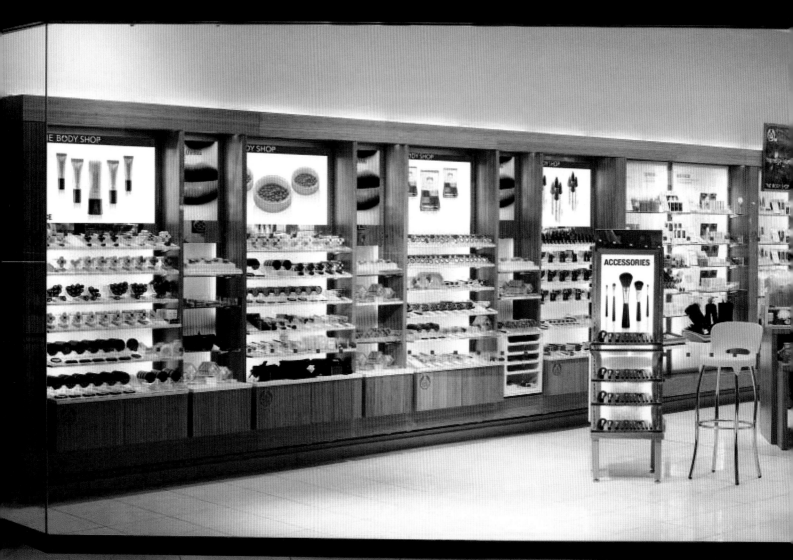

Skin and hair care items are the forte of The Body Shop, whose 600-plus products and more than 400 accessories are sold in over 2,000 outlets worldwide.

The Body Shop was founded in 1976 by Anita Roddick when she started selling homemade naturally inspired products with minimal packaging. Her first store, in Brighton on England's south coast, offered only 25 hand-mixed products. The Body Shop later brought unheard-of products to upscale British retailing — aloe vera, jojoba oil, rhassoil mud and cocoa butter, to name a few. A kiosk in Brussels two years later became the company's first overseas franchise. The company went public in 1985.

The company estimates it sells more than two products per second, day and night, somewhere on the globe, to its 77 million customers — best sellers include Vitamin E Moisture Cream, Tea Tree Oil and Banana Shampoo.

Identified with environmental and animal protection since its inception, The Body Shop's adopted causes over the years have included Save the Whales with Greenpeace, the burning of the Brazilian rainforest, renewable energy, human rights and, in 1996, the United Kingdom's passage of the first ban on animal testing for cosmetic products and ingredients. The Body Shop Foundation was launched in 1990 and The Body Shop Human Rights Award in 2000.

Building social activism into the company's business, The Body Shop has launched a Community Trade Program that creates sustainable trading relationships with disadvantaged communities around the world, now including 35 suppliers from some 25 countries. The program seeks to build livelihoods, support sustainable developments and provide health and educational benefits in those nations. Roddick has also established the New Academy of Business at The University of Bath, adding social, environmental and ethical issues to managerial studies.

*Founded in 1976, The Body Shop sells 600-plus natural skin and hair care products in over 2,000 outlets worldwide.*

©Vismedia

©Vismedia

©Vismedia

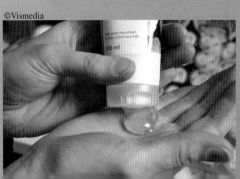

# Boots

| | |
|---|---|
| **Parent Company/ Corporate Name:** | **The Boots Group PLC** |
| Corporate Retail Headquarters: | The Boots Group PLC 1 Thane Road West Nottingham NG2 3AA, United Kingdom +44-115-950-6111 www.boots-plc.com |
| Annual Revenue: | $8.7 billion (2004) |
| Countries of Operation: | 130 |
| Retail Classification: | Drugstore, specialty |

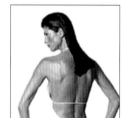

*The Boots Group manufacturers and sells health and personal care products through three divisions.*

The Boots Group manufactures and sells health and personal care products. It operates through three divisions — Boots Retail, Boots Retail International and Boots Healthcare International.

Boots Retail contains the company's operations in Ireland (59 stores) and the U.K. Boots the Chemist sells over 2,000 lines of health and beauty products through its 1,400 stores. Boots offers "well-being services" that include optical, hearing, and foot care services; some of these are available via the Internet as well.

Boots Retail International oversees operations in The Netherlands (Etos stores), Italy (Esselunga supermarkets), Taiwan (A.S. Watson stores) and Thailand (Tops Supermarkets)

Boots Healthcare International focuses on three categories of therapies: skin care, analgesics and cough and cold. Its acquisition of Clearasil has extended its presence in the U.S. and Japan, and it offers its pain relief gels in the U.K., Australia, New Zealand and The Netherlands.

Boots' roots can be traced to 1849, when John Boot opened The British and American Botanic Establishment at 6 Goose Gate, where he provided physical comfort for the needy, perhaps using techniques learned from his mother, who had used herbs in healing. His 10-year-old son, Jesse, got behind the counter after his father's death and brought the company into its own over the next 50 years. In the latter part of the twentieth century, Boots focused on product development and introduction of new services. Today, Boots is committed to three principles: customer convenience, good locations and the "right offer" to its customers.

*"Wellbeing services" that include optical, hearing and footcare are available.*

*Boots is committed to three principles: customer convenience, good locations and the "right offer" to its customers.*

# Borders Group, Inc.

**BORDERS**
GROUP

---

| | |
|---|---|
| **Parent Company/ Corporate Name:** | **Borders Group, Inc.** |
| Corporate Retail Headquarters: | 100 Phoenix Drive Ann Arbor, MI 48108, United States 734-477-1100 www.bordersgroupinc.com |
| Annual Revenue: | $3.9 billion (2004) |
| Number of Locations: | 1,200 |
| Countries of Operation: | The U.S., the U.K., Singapore, New Zealand, Australia |
| Retail Classification: | Specialty |

*B orders Group has more than 1,200 Borders and Waldenbooks stores around the world. Online shopping is also available through two websites.*

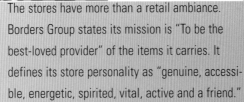

Borders Group has more than 1,200 Borders and Waldenbooks stores around the world. Its chains include about 450 Borders superstores in the U.S.; 37 Borders stores outside the U.S., principally in the U.K. and the Pacific Rim; 36 Books etc. stores in the U.K.; and about 700 Waldenbooks stores in the U.S. Online shopping is available through two websites.

The stores have more than a retail ambiance. Borders Group states its mission is "To be the best-loved provider" of the items it carries. It defines its store personality as "genuine, accessible, energetic, spirited, vital, active and a friend."

Borders stores offer more than books, including music, movies and other entertainment items (which account for much of the chain's attraction to younger shoppers). The Borders stores offer cozy chairs, comfortable cafes and listening stations so customers can relax and stay awhile. Shoppers can track down their sought-after books on Title Sleuth computer kiosks. The Waldenbooks stores are a mall-based book retailer, with stores in all 50 states.

A single book-rental library, founded in 1933 in Bridgeport, Connecticut, grew into the Walden Book Stores. The Borders brothers, Tom and Louis, opened Borders Books in 1971 in the college town of Ann Arbor, Michigan. Both brands were bought by discount retailer Kmart in 1994. The remaining stock was purchased back from Kmart in 1995 and the new company went public on the New York Stock Exchange.

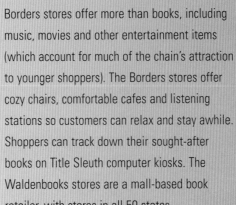

*In addition to books, Borders stores offer music, movies and other entertainment items, which attract younger shoppers.*

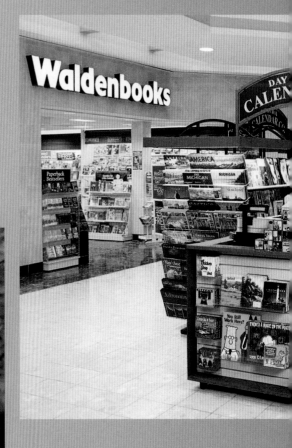

# Build-A-Bear Workshop, Inc.

| | |
|---|---|
| **Parent Company/ Corporate Name:** | **Build-A-Bear Workshop, Inc.** |
| Corporate Retail Headquarters: | 1954 Innerbelt Center Drive St. Louis, MO 63114, United States 314 423 8000 www.buildabear.com |
| Annual Revenue: | $301.7 million (2004) |
| Number of Locations: | 190 |
| Countries of Operation: | The U.S., Canada, the U.K., Japan, Denmark, Australia, South Korea, France |
| Retail Classification: | Toys |

*B*uild-A-Bear workshops contain bear-making stations where customers design their own teddy bears and other stuffed animals complete with clothing and accessories.

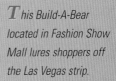 HUGGABLE HEROES™

Build-A-Bear Workshop, Where Best Friends Are Made, is an interactive retail experience built on the affection of people of all ages for stuffed animals, particularly teddy bears. Launched in the Saint Louis Galleria in October 1997, by founder Maxine Clark, the company has expanded to retail operations to four continents. The store's mascot is Bearemy®, a 6'4" teddy whose love for honey has made him "beary shy" about his weight.

Each store contains bear-making stations. At "Choose Me," the customer selects one of a range of furry options, including teddy bears, bunnies, dogs, kitties, frogs and ponies. At the "Hear Me" station, the shopper adds a sound choice to place inside the animal, or records and inserts a unique sound. Stuffing is added at "Stuff Me." A small satin heart is gained at "Heart Stuff," and at "Stitch Me," the last seam is pulled shut. The process continues with fluffing and naming. Clothing from formalwear to Western wear can be chosen, and accessories include eyewear, cellphones and sporting goods. The process ends when the customer receives the bear's "birth certificate."

There are many corporate tie-ins with the bears. Bear-sized Limited Too fashions are available, as are Skechers shoes and apparel from Major League Baseball, NBA and WBNA teams. A co-branding partnership with the World Wildlife Fund generates funds for that charity, and other animal-related organizations benefit from the bears as well.

A Stuffed With Hugs program sends special teddy bears to children in need worldwide. Read Teddy encourages children's literacy.

Guests can plan and customize a party with pre-selected animals, clothes and accessories, or can select bears and accoutrements at the company's website. In 2005, the company launched a 40,000-mile national tour with a 53-foot trailer containing a complete 800 sq. ft. Build-A-Bear Workshop store.

*T*his Build-A-Bear located in Fashion Show Mall lures shoppers off the Las Vegas strip.

WE MAKE BEARY GOOD FRIENDS

# Burberry

**BURBERRY**

| | |
|---|---|
| **Parent Company/ Corporate Name:** | Burberry Group plc |
| Corporate Retail Headquarters: | 18-22 Haymarket London SW1 4DQ, United Kingdom +44-207-968-0000 www.burberry.com |
| Annual Revenue: | £715 million (2005) |
| Number of Locations: | 230 |
| Countries of Operation: | Europe, the U.S., South America, Asia, the Middle East |
| Retail Classification: | Specialty |

*Burberry has long been associated with it's gabardine-checked fabric, invented by founder Thomas Burberry.*

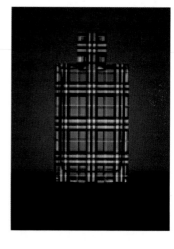

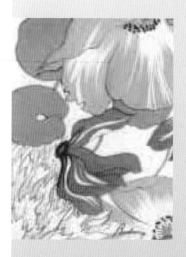

Burberry has long been associated with its gabardine-checked fabric, invented by founder Thomas Burberry, and Burberry-lined "trench" coats, worn by British soldiers in WWI, became a company icon. Burberry operates retail and wholesale businesses and a licensing network. Its 230-plus company-owned stores and concessions in high-end department stores worldwide sell men's and women's designer apparel and accessories under the Prorsum, Burberry London, and Thomas Burberry names. Burberry has recently experienced a fashion renaissance and has expanded into baby clothes, blue jeans, and personal products.

Burberry is a luxury brand with a distinctive British sensibility, strong international recognition and differentiating brand values that resonate across a multi-generational and dual-gender audience. The company designs and source apparel and accessories distributing through a diversified network of retail, wholesale and licensing channels worldwide.

©Ilan Rubin

*The company sells men's and women's designer apparel and accessories through its company-owned stores and high-end department store concessions worldwide.*

# C&A

| Parent Company/<br>Corporate Name: | **COFRA Holding AG** |
|---|---|
| Corporate Retail<br>Headquarters: | Senneberg, Jean Monnetlaan<br>Vilvoorde, Belgium<br>+32-22576064<br>www.c-and-a.com |
| Annual Revenue: | $6.2 billion (2004) |
| Number of Locations: | 648 |
| Countries of Operation: | Austria, Belgium, the Czech Republic, France, Germany,<br>Hungary, Luxembourg, The Netherlands, Poland, Portugal,<br>Spain, Switzerland |
| Retail Classification: | Specialty |

C&A calls itself "Europe's house of clothing . . . for the entire family." Its 648 stores offer a variety of price ranges and 11 exclusive brands, including Angelo Litrico, Clockhouse, Jinglers, Yessica, Westbury and Your Sixth Sense. Over 460 designers and buyers determine the brands' portfolios, which cover the trendy to the classic for men, women, teenagers and children.

C&A is a family-operated company, and the men of the Brenninkmeijer founding family still hold most senior management posts. Family is a theme, as shown by its own statement that "C&A is a company characterized by values that are

also important aspects of family life," most notably a long-term approach to things and lasting relations at all levels, including customers, suppliers, employees and others.

C&A's 20 Clockhouse shops focus on activewear for teenagers, while its 92 Kids Stores feature apparel for pre-teens.

C&A takes its name from the initials of the German brothers Clemens and August Brenninkmeijer, who founded a textile warehouse under the C&A name in The Netherlands in 1841. The first store opened in 1861, and was a great success, as one of the first outlets anywhere to offer ready-to-wear at prices that were affordable to the workingman.

*C &A's 648 stores offer a variety of price ranges and 11 exclusive brands.*

*The company's 20 Clockhouse shops focus on activewear for teenagers, while its 92 Kids Stores feature apparel for pre-teens.*

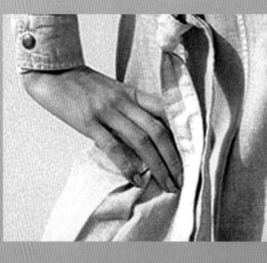

# Carrefour

**Parent Company/
Corporate Name:** **Carrefour**

Corporate Retail
Headquarters:
6 avenue Raymond Poincare
Paris 75016, France
+33-1-53-70-19-00
www.carrefour.com

Annual Revenue: $89.6 billion (2004)

Number of Locations: 6,067

Countries of Operation: 29, throughout Europe, Asia, Africa, the Americas

Retail Classification: Hypermarkets, supermarkets, discount, convenience,
food service

*T*he Carrefour
hypermarkets offer a
wide range of food and
non-food products at
attractive prices.

Carrefour's 6,067 stores in 29 countries cross categories, including 750 hypermarkets, 1,471 supermarkets, 3,510 discount stores, 165 convenience stores and 171 cash-and-carry. The hypermarket, supermarket and hard discount formats are in rapid expansion beyond France.

The Carrefour hypermarkets offer a wide range of food and nonfood products at attractive prices. Their shelves stock an average of 70,000 items. Floor areas range from 50,000 to over 200,000 square feet. Of the 750, 178 are in France and 119 in Spain.

The supermarkets go under the names Champion, GS, Norte, Gb and Marinopoulos. They offer a wide selection of mostly food products at competitive prices, in stores that range in size from 10,000 to 20,000 square feet.

Hard discounters such as Dia, Ed and Minipreço stock 800 food products at very reasonable prices in small stores (less than 8,000 square feet). Half the products are sold under the Dia brand name.

Convenience stores include the Shopi, Marché Plus, 8 à Huit and Di per Di chains. The cash-and-carry and food service outlets are designed to meet the needs of restaurant and food industry professionals.

The Carrefour group was founded in 1959. Its first supermarket opened the next year in Annecy, Haute-Savoie. Carrefour's hypermarket concept debuted in 1963 in the Paris suburbs. Spain's first Carrefour hypermarket opened 11 years later. In 2002, the group opened its first hypermarket in Japan.

*C*arrefour's 6,067 stores in 29 countries include hypermarkets, supermarkets, discount stores, convenience stores and cash-and-carry.

# Casino Guichard-Perrachon S.A.

| | |
|---|---|
| **Parent Company/ Corporate Name:** | Rallye S.A. |
| Corporate Retail Headquarters: | 24, rue de la Montat 42008 Saint-Etienne, France +33-4-77-45-31-31 www.groupe-casino.fr |
| Annual Revenue: | $28 billion (2004) |
| Number of Locations: | 8,600 |
| Countries of Operation: | Brazil, France, Colombia, Madagascar, The Netherlands, Poland, Taiwan, Thailand, the U.S., Venezuela |
| Retail Classification: | Hypermarket, supermarket, discount, convenience, restaurants |

*I ts supermarkets operate under at least 16 names throughout the world, including Casino and Franprix in France and Super De Boer in The Netherlands.*

Casino operates about 8,600 stores in a range of formats: hypermarkets, supermarkets and convenience stores, among others.

Its hypermarkets are found in France, Brazil, Thailand, Colombia, and elsewhere under the names Extra, Big C, Géant, Exito, and Optimo.

Casino's 2,264 supermarkets operate under at least 16 names worldwide. The 1,220 in France are Casino and Franprix. In The Netherlands, one will find 369 Super De Boer supermarkets and 90 Konmar supermarkets. The 230 in the U.S. operate as Smart & Final and United Grocers, and the 211 in Brazil are called Pão de Açúcar.

Casino is a major convenience store operator in France, with 4,568 stores, mostly under the Petit Casino name, but also as Vival.

Its 945 discount stores can be found as Leader Price in France (370 stores) and Poland (133 stores), Edah in The Netherlands (269 stores) and Barateiro in Brazil (169 stores).

*C*asino owns and operates about 8,600 hypermarkets, supermarkets, convenience stores and discount stores worldwide.

# Coach

| Parent Company/<br>Corporate Name: | Coach, Inc. |
|---|---|
| Corporate Retail<br>Headquarters: | 516 W. 34th Street<br>New York, NY 10001<br>United States<br>(212) 594-1850<br>www.coach.com |
| Annual Revenue: | $1.7 billion (2005) |
| Number of Locations: | 287 |
| Countries of Operation: | The U.S. and 18 other countries |
| Retail Classification: | Apparel |

*Coach products are crafted from natural leather and feature signature details such as distinctive hardware and stitching.*

*The company, founded in 1941, also licenses its name for furniture, footwear and watches.*

Coach designs and produces classically styled, high-quality leather goods and accessories for men and women, including luggage, purses, outerwear and gloves.

Coach products are glove-tanned pieces crafted from natural leather that burnishes over time, acquiring a rich, lustrous patina. From handbags to backpacks, each style features signature details such as distinctive hardware, double-needle stitching and bound edges. The shapes soften gradually to the touch, taking on the individual imprint of the wearer.

The Business Collection features a broad range of pieces, including briefcases, organizers, planners, notepads, computer cases and cellphone cases. Function is paramount, as is an understated sophistication.

The Travel Collection is a luxurious assortment of highly durable and functional luggage and travel accessories in leather and lightweight travel twill created to address the diverse needs of business and weekend travelers. Beyond these collections, Coach offers a variety of handbags and accessories encompassing a wide range of materials and updated designs.

Founded in 1941, the company also licenses its name for watches, footwear and furniture. In addition to 285 stores and factory-outlets in the United States and two in the United Kingdom, Coach sells its wares through department stores in the United States and in 18 other countries, via catalogs and through its Web site. Current plans are to open approximately 20 new stores a year.

©Mark Milian

# Coop Norden

| | |
|---|---|
| **Parent Company/**<br>**Corporate Name:** | **Kooperativa Forbundet Group (KF)/FDB/**<br>**Coop NKL BA Sweden** |
| Corporate Retail<br>Headquarters: | Kungsgatan 49<br>101 20 Stockholm, Sweden<br>+46-8-743-54-00<br>www.coopnorden.com |
| Annual Revenue: | $11.8 billion (2004) |
| Number of Locations: | 1,080 |
| Countries of Operation: | Denmark, Norway, Sweden |
| Retail Classification: | Hypermarkets, supermarkets, convenience, discount |

*S*tructured as a consumer cooperative, Coop Norden owns and/or operates locations throughout Denmark, Norway and Sweden.

Coop Norden owns and/or operates locations throughout Denmark, Norway and Sweden. It is structured as a consumer cooperative. Its parent companies are actually three associations: Kooperativa Forbundet Group (KF), which owns 42%; FDB, which owns 38%; and Coop Norge, which owns 20%.

Coop Norden was formed in 2002 through the merger of its three subdivisions: Coop Danmark, Coop Norge and Coop Sverige. Its 1,000 outlets employ about 28,000 people.

Its minimarts in Denmark are known as Dagli'Brugsen and SuperBrugsen, and in Norway as Coop Norden. The stores offer food and non-food items, as well as personal services such as post office branches.

The company's supermarkets are SuperBrugsen (Denmark), Irma (Copenhagen, Denmark), Coop Mega (Norway), and Coop Konsum and Coop Extra in Sweden. Their stores are the largest supermarket chains in Denmark and Norway.

Its hypermarkets are Kvickly (Denmark), Coop Obs! and its do-it-yourself partner, Coop Obs! Bygg, (Norway) and Coop Forum (Sweden).

Its discount operations include Fakta (Denmark) and Coop Prix (Norway).

*C*oop Norden stores offer food and non-food items, as well as personal services such as post office branches.

# Costco Wholesale

| | |
|---|---|
| **Parent Company/ Corporate Name:** | **Costco Wholesale Corporation** |
| Corporate Retail Headquarters: | 999 Lake Drive Issaquah, WA 98027, United States 425-313-8100 www.costco.com |
| Annual Revenue: | $47.1 billion (2004) |
| Number of Locations: | 441 |
| Countries of Operation: | The U.S., Canada, Mexico, Japan, England, Scotland, Taiwan, Korea |
| Retail Classification: | Membership Wholesale Club |

*W*arehouses offer discount prices on products ranging from fresh food and alcoholic beverages to appliances and toys.

Costco operates a chain of membership warehouses that sell high-quality, nationally branded and selected private-label merchandise at low prices to business purchasing for commercial use, personal use, or resale, and also to individuals who are members of selected employee groups.

The company's U.S. operations include 441 warehouses in 36 states and Puerto Rico. Its foreign presence consists of 62 stores in nine Canadian provinces, 15 U.K. locations, 5 in Korea, 4 in Japan, 3 through a subsidiary in Taiwan and 23 in Mexico through a joint venture.

Costco made its debut in 1983, with a warehouse in Seattle, Washington. It opened 19 new warehouses in 2003 alone, 6 in new markets and 13 in established markets.

The company is exploring new approaches. A Costco Home warehouse opened in Kirkland, Washington, in 2002, offering high-end furniture and accessories with typical Costco prices. It has recently expanded its small chain of Costco

Business Centers. Special-order kiosks debuted in 2002, providing Costco's members access to hundreds of additional upscale items.

Costco has over 20 million members, representing over 40 million cardholders. Over 2 million are "executive members" who pay $100 per year to take advantage of over 20 special services and discounts, including an annual percentage "reward" based on purchase volume.

The company publishes a member directory, explaining services such as auto and home insurance, roadside assistance, mortgage and refinancing services, financial planning and medical savings cards. Its monthly magazine, *The Costco Connection,* offers a calendar of items available at specific Costco locations for a limited time only, and articles related to member services.

*C*ostco's chain of membership warehouses sells high-quality, nationally branded merchandise at low prices.

©*Mark Milian*

# Dairy Farm International

| | |
|---|---|
| **Parent Company/ Corporate Name:** | **Dairy Farm International** |
| Corporate Retail Headquarters: | 7/F Devon House, Taikoo Place 979 King's Road, P.O. Box 286, GPO Quarry Bay, Hong Kong +852-2299-1888 www.dairyfarmgroup.com |
| Annual Revenue: | $4 billion (2004) |
| Number of Locations: | 2,570 |
| Countries of Operation: | Hong Kong, Taiwan, China, Singapore, Malaysia, Indonesia, India, South Korea |
| Retail Classification: | Supermarket, hypermarket, specialty, drug, convenience |

*D airy Farm has grown to a chain of 2,570 hypermarkets, supermarkets, convenience and specialty stores serving much of the Pacific Rim.*

Scottish surgeon Sir Patrick Manson and five Hong Kong businessmen started Dairy Farm in 1886 to improve the health of Hong Kong's people by supplying them with cows' milk kept free from contamination through stringent hygiene and, further, to import a herd of dairy cows to cut the price of milk in half.

In the years since, Dairy Farm has grown to a chain of 2,570 supermarkets, convenience stores, hypermarkets, specialty stores and drug stores throughout the Pacific Rim, except for Japan.

Today, Dairy Farm emphasizes value for money through low-cost efficient distribution of high-quality foods and consumer and durable goods. It is geographically committed to Asia and plans to explore new investment opportunities within the region.

Its supermarket chains include Wellcome in Hong Kong and Taiwan, Cold Storage in Singapore and Malaysia, Giant in Malaysia, Shop N Save in Singapore, Hero in Indonesia and Foodworld in India.

Its Giant hypermarket chain serves Malaysia, Singapore and Indonesia. Its health and beauty stores throughout the region go under Mannings, Guardian, Health and Glow and Olive Young.

Its convenience stores are 7-Eleven in Hong Kong, Singapore and Southern China and Starmart in Indonesia. It also operates IKEA in Hong Kong and Taiwan, and holds half-interest in Maxim's, Hong Kong's leading restaurant chain.

0 - Present

0 - Present

0 - Present

*S tores offer low-cost efficient distribution of high-quality foods and consumer and durable goods.*

# Debenhams

DEBENHAMS

| Parent Company/ Corporate Name: | Debenhams |
|---|---|
| Corporate Retail Headquarters: | 1 Welbeck Street London W1G 0AA, United Kingdom +44-20-7428-4444 www.debenhams.com |
| Annual Revenue: | $3.4 billion (2004) |
| Number of Locations: | 102 |
| Countries of Operation: | Cyprus, the Czech Republic, Denmark, the U.K., United Arab Emirates, Iceland, Indonesia, Kuwait, Malaysia, Quatar, Saudi Arabia, Sharjah, Sweden |
| Retail Classification: | Department store |

*D*ebenhams focuses on fashion for women, men and children, as well as offering cosmetics and housewares.

Debenhams department store focuses on fashion, serving women, men and children, as well as offering cosmetics and housewares. The company dates back to 1778, with the Debenhams name first appearing in 1813. Its retail outlets and clothing manufacturing operations grew throughout the nineteenth century and the first Debenhams department store opened in 1905.

In the late 1980s, Debenhams' management introduced exclusive ranges of own-brand merchandise including "Designers at Debenhams." Its brand list includes J, Pearce II Fionda, Philip Treacy, BDL, Lulu Guiness, ROCHA and G. Its housewares department has launched into designer products with Jane Asher cookware. The company also offers a wedding gift service and in-store restaurants and cafes.

Debenhams sells over 500 international brands, and is the U.K.'s number-one retailer of many of them, including Estée Lauder, Clinique, Clarins, Meyer, Portmeirion, Viners-Oneids, Ben Sherman, Playtex and Lepel.

The company reports good recent growth in other product lines, including gifts, board games and technical gadgets.

Debenhams now operates 102 stores in the U.K. and Ireland. It also has a network of franchised stores in Cyprus, the Czech Republic, Denmark, Dubai, Iceland, Indonesia, Kuwait, Malaysia, Qatar, Saudi Arabia, Sharjah and Sweden. In 2003 the company received the Retail Week Award for Overseas Initiative.

*T*he company operates 102 stores in the U.K. and has a network of franchised stores in other areas which include Bahrain, Denmark and Malaysia.

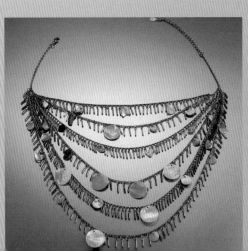

# Delhaize Group

| | |
|---|---|
| **Parent Company/**<br>**Corporate Name:** | **Delhaize Group** |
| Corporate Retail<br>Headquarters: | Rue Osseghemstraat 53<br>Brussels 1080, Belgium<br>+32-2-412-21-11<br>www.delhaizegroup.com |
| Annual Revenue: | $22.3 billion (2004) |
| Number of Locations: | 2,614 |
| Countries of Operation: | Belgium, the Czech Republic, Germany, Grand-Duchy of<br>Luxembourg, Greece, Indonesia, Romania, Thailand, the U.S. |
| Retail Classification: | Supermarket, convenience |

*T he Delhaize Group operates supermarkets, neighborhood stores and specialty shops in North America, Europe and Southeast Asia.*

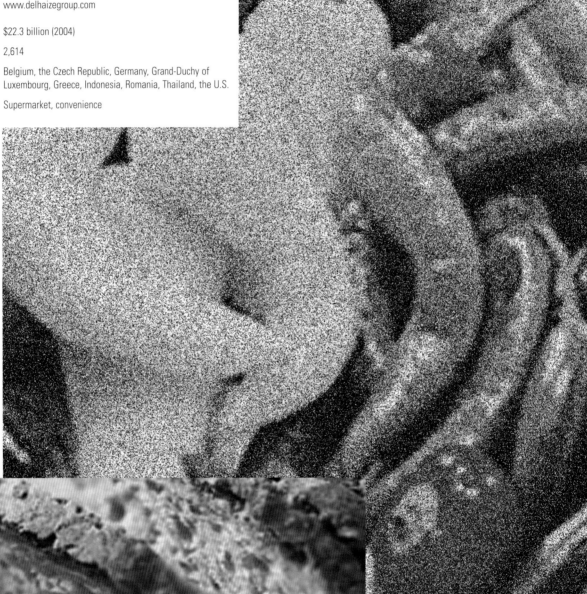

For more than 100 years, "Le Lion" has symbolized the Delhaize Group, which was founded by Professor Louis Delhaize in Belgium in 1867. Delhaize Group operates supermarkets in North America, Europe and Southeast Asia. In addition to supermarkets, which account for about 85% of its sales network, Delhaize Group includes other store formats such as neighborhood stores, specialty shops and convenience stores.

Delhaize Group also engages in food wholesaling to stores in its sales network and in nonfood retailing of pet, health and beauty products.

The company seeks "to be one of the most admired international food retailers by its customers." To do so, it works to achieve leading positions both in key mature and emerging markets through strong local chains.

Present in the U.S. since the mid-1950s, Delhaize Group operates under the banners Food Lion (1,213 stores in 11 Southeast states), Hannaford Bros. (122 supermarkets in New England and New York), Kash n' Karry (103 stores in Florida) and Harveys (43 supermarkets in south and central Georgia).

In Belgium, the company's historical home, the Delhaize Group sales network comprises 728 stores. Le Lion supermarkets is its banner there, but the chain also includes the AD Delhaize

supermarkets, the Proxy Delhaize convenience stores, the Shop 'n Go gas station convenience stores, the Delhaize City neighborhood stores and the Caddy-Home business-to-consumer operation that sells food products by telephone, fax and the Internet.

Elsewhere, the company's stores are known as Alfa-Beta (Greece), Delvita (the Czech Republic and Slovakia), Mega Image (Romania), Food Lion (Thailand) and Super Indo (Indonesia).

*T*he company sells under the Le Lion and AD Delhaize banners in Belgium and the Food Lion and Hannaford banners in the U.S.

# DSG International plc

**Dixons** **The Link** **HELKJØP** **mastercare** **PC WORLD** THE COMPUTER SUPERSTORE **Currys**

**Parent Company/
Corporate Name:** **Dixons Group plc**

Corporate Retail
Headquarters:
Dixons House, Maylands Avenue
Hemel Hempstead
Hertfordshire HP2 7TG, United Kingdom
+44-1442-353-000
www.dixons-group-plc.co.uk

Annual Revenue: $12.1 billion (2004)

Countries of Operation: The U.K. and 11 other European countries

Retail Classification: Specialty, discount

*Dixons Group stores specialize in high-technology items, consumer electronics, personal computers, photographic equipment and communication products.*

Dixons Group was founded in 1937 by Charles Kalms as a small photographic studio. Ready to open, Kalms and his partner Michael Mindel found that the shop front could only accommodate a sign six letters long. A solution was found in the telephone directory under "D."

The company flourished in World War II, which brought an unprecedented demand for portrait photography, particularly of servicemen and their families. After the war, the company shrank as

fast as it had grown. It turned to marketing new and used photographic products and subsequently became a mail order business. In the 1980s, the company acquired a number of other chains.

Since then, Dixons Group stores have specialized in high-technology items, consumer electronics, personal computers, domestic appliances, photographic equipment and communication products. Its stores are known as Dixons (204 U.K. stores), PC World (which includes in-store clinics), PC City, The Link (284 U.K. stores), Mastercare Service, Electro World and UniEuro. Its Currys chain, the U.K.'s largest electrical retailer, has nearly 300 superstores and 84 high street stores there.

Overall, the group has more than 1,400 stores throughout the U.K., France, Spain, Italy, the Nordic countries, Hungary and the Czech Republic. The Group launched its first tax-free Dixons store at Heathrow Airport in 1994 and now has 18 airport stores.

*T*here are more than 1,400 stores throughout Europe.

*Photos: Reprinted with permission from DSG International plc*

# dm-drogeriemarkt

**Parent Company/
Corporate Name:**          dm-drogeriemarkt

Corporate Retail
Headquarters:              Carl-Metz-Strasse 1
                           Karlsruhhe 76185, Germany
                           +49-0721-5592-0
                           www.dm-drogeriemarkt.de

Annual Revenue:            $3.4 billion (2004)
Number of Locations:       1,431

Countries of Operation:    Germany, Austria, Croatia, the Czech Republic, Hungary, Italy,
                           the Slovak Republic, Slovenia

Retail Classification:     Drugstore

*d*m-drogeriemarkt offers a wide range of items including cosmetics, baby, health and beauty products.

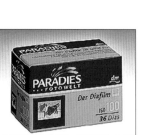

A successful drugstore chain in Europe, dm-drogeriemarkt, has over 1,400 stores in eight countries. It estimates that over one-half million people shop at dm stores each day, buying up to 1,300 items per store per day.

Founded in 1973 by Götz Werner, dm-drogeriemarkt offers a wide range of consumer products in many lines — baby, cosmetics, photo, health and beauty, and others.

*W*ith over 1,400 stores in eight countries, dm-drogeriemarkt is among the most successful drugstore chains in Europc.

# Edeka Zentrale

**Parent Company/
Corporate Name:**     Edeka Zentrale AG

**Corporate Retail
Headquarters:**     New York Ring 6
D22297 Hamburg, Germany
+49-40-63770
www.edeka.de

**Annual Revenue:**     $32.1 billion (2004)

**Countries of Operation:**     Germany, Austria, the Czech Republic, Denmark, France, Poland

**Retail Classification:**     Food service, drugstores, hypermarkets

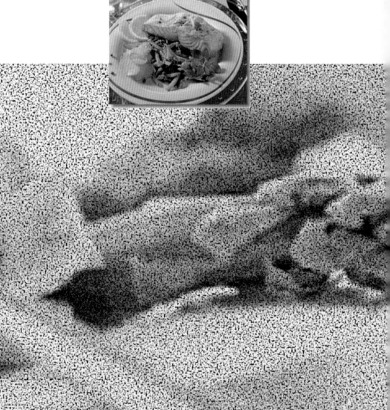

*E*deka Zentrale is one of Europe's largest retail and wholesale food organizations.

One of the largest retail and wholesale food groups in Europe, Edeka Zentrale is a consortium of 15 cooperatives. It comprises 120,000 largely independent retailers. Edeka offers them a wide range of dairy, cereals, fruits and vegetables. Major brands include SPAR, Bio Wertkost, Rio Grande and Mibell.

Edeka also includes drugstores, food processing operations, a banking subsidiary and a publishing house. Edeka owns a majority interest in AVA, a German hypermarket retailer with about 400 stores, and in the German grocery chain Otto Reichelt.

*E*deka offers a wide range of products. Major brands include Rio Grande, Bio Wertkost, SPAR and Mibell.

Frisch aus der Backstube

Das Bio-Sortiment der EDEKA

So schmeckt Italien

Alles für Hund, Katz' & Co.

Kostbarkeiten aus der Schlemmer Küche

Zug um Zug – preiswert genießen

Die Marke für Kosmetik und Körperpflege

Knackiges aus der Gemüse Küche

Das Qualitätsfleisch von EDEKA

KING'S GOLD für jede Gelegenheit

Die Geflügelspezialitäten von EDEKA

Lomita für smarte Raucher

Das Technik-Sortiment von EDEKA

Die Marke rund um Frucht und Frühstück

# E. Leclerc

| | |
|---|---|
| **Parent Company/ Corporate Name:** | E. Leclerc |
| Corporate Retail Headquarters: | 52 rue Camille Desmoulins 92451 Issy-les-Moulineaux, France +33-1-46-62-51-00 www.e-leclerc.com |
| Annual Revenue: | $34.8 billion (2004) |
| Countries of Operation: | France, Poland, Portugal, Spain, Slovenia |
| Retail Classification: | Food service, specialty, supermarkets, hypermarkets, others |

*The federation's members benefit from Leclerc's purchasing power and sell local goods as well.*

Established in 1949, E. Leclerc is a federation of independent food retailers with a central management office in Paris and 16 regional offices. It supports about 560 separately owned hypermarkets and supermarkets — a majority operating with the Galec name in France. It also has members in Portugal, Poland, Spain and Slovenia.

The federation's members benefit from E. Leclerc's purchasing power and also sell local goods to preserve their image as community businesses.

A retailer wishing to join the cooperative must take part in a training program, may not own more than two stores, and must spend a portion of his or her time working for the cooperative itself.

Its hypermarkets offer jewelry, dining, auto service, pharmacies and travel services. Leclerc is France's biggest jeweler and the nation's second-largest bookstore.

*Among France's largest food retailers, E. Leclerc supports about 560 separately owned hypermarkets and supermarkets.*

# The Estée Lauder Companies Inc.

| Parent Company/ Corporate Name: | The Estée Lauder Companies Inc. |
| --- | --- |
| Corporate Retail Headquarters: | 767 Fifth Avenue New York, NY 10153-0023, United States 212-572-4200 www.elcompanies.com |
| Annual Revenue: | $6.3 billion (2005) |
| Countries of Operation: | 130 worldwide |
| Retail Classification: | Beauty |

*Estée Lauder cosmetics, fragrances and skin care products are sold worldwide under brand names including Estée Lauder, Clinique, Origins, Aveda and M-A-C.*

# AVEDA

Estée Lauder has been synonymous with beauty since the company's founding in 1946. Mrs. Lauder was armed with just four products and her unmistakable belief that every woman can be beautiful.

In short order, her company — founded on skin care products — expanded into fragrances and other beauty items. The company's brands include skin care items Estée Lauder, Aramis and Clinique; the urban Prescriptives; Origins, the company's lifestyle brand; and the La Mer skin care treatments. It owns makeup artist lines M-A-C, Bobbi Brown and Stila. Other beauty lines include Aveda, a maker of hair, skin and make-up products created from natural ingredients, Bumble and bumble, American Beauty, Flirt!, good skin, grassroots, and Donald Trump, the fragrance. Its best-known scent is the legendary Youth-Dew.

Estée Lauder stores in the Americas account for 55% of company sales. The company established its first European store in 1960 in London. Europe, Africa and the Mideast account for 32% of sales. Asia joined the Estée Lauder network in 1963 with a presence in Hong Kong, and now accounts for 13% of sales.

Now represented in over 130 countries, the Estée Lauder Companies is today run by her family, offering 9,000 products, with 300 new items added each year.

*Represented in over 130 countries, the Estée Lauder Companies offer 9,000 products, with 300 new items added each year.*

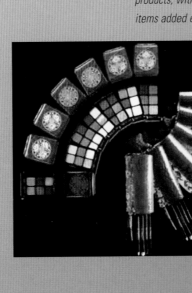

# Fast Retailing

| | |
|---|---|
| **Parent Company/ Corporate Name:** | **Fast Retailing** |
| Corporate Retail Headquarters: | 717-1 Oaza Sayama Yamaguchi, 754-0894, Japan +81-83-988-0333 www.uniqlo.co.jp |
| Annual Revenue: | $3 billion (2004) |
| Number of Locations: | 600 |
| Countries of Operation: | Japan, China, the U.K, the U.S. |
| Retail Classification: | Specialty |

*Fast Retailing is one of Japan's fastest growing chains of casual clothing for men, women and children.*

Fast Retailing is one of Japan's fastest growing chains of casual clothing for children and men and women of all ages. It is known for its UNIQLO Stores. (UNIQLO combines the Japanese words for "unique" and "clothing.") UNIQLO's unisex casualwear is known for its good quality and palette of primary colors. It is often compared to the Gap brand.

The company seeks to "provide fashionable, high quality basic casualwear at the lowest prices in the market — casualwear that anybody can wear whenever and wherever." It achieves that goal through low cost operation and the "shortest and cheapest means" of linking production and marketing. The company keeps tight control of all production stages, from planning and fabric development to manufacturing, distribution and sales.

Fast Retailing/Uniqlo dates from 1949, when Men's Shop Ogori Shoji opened in Ube City, Yamaguchi Prefecture, Japan. The first UNIQLO store, specializing in casual clothing, opened in 1974. Ogori Shoji changed its name to Fast Retailing in 1991. A growth spurt from 1994–1996 doubled the number of stores to 200, increasing to over 507 direct-run stores by 2001. Online Internet selling started in 2000.

Four stores in the U.K. debuted in 2001, with two stores in Shanghai, China, opening the following year. A subsidiary, FR Foods Co., Ltd., was also established in 2002. In 2005, four UNIQLO stores were opened in the U.S.

*U NIQLO stores specialize in casual wear that is known for its good quality and palette of primary colors.*

# Foot Locker

| | |
|---|---|
| **Parent Company/ Corporate Name:** | **Foot Locker, Inc.** |
| Corporate Retail Headquarters: | 112 West 34th Street New York, NY 10120, United States 212-720-3700 www.footlocker-inc.com |
| Annual Revenue: | $5.3 billion (2005) |
| Number of Locations: | 4,000 |
| Countries of Operation: | 11, throughout North America, Europe, Asia, Australia |
| Retail Classification: | Specialty |

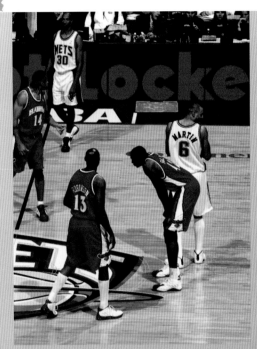

IF Foot Locker, Inc. is leader in the athletic footwear and sports apparel industry. Its divisions include Foot Locker, Lady Foot Locker and Kids Foot Locker.

With nearly 4,000 stores, the chain also includes Champs Sports (athletic wear), Eastbay (a catalog retailer) and a website, www.footlocker.com. It operated for many years under the name Venator Group, taken from the Latin word meaning "sportsman" or "hunter." Foot Locker's sponsorship programs with the professional basketball, baseball and hockey associations guarantee high visibility among sports fans.

An industry was launched when the first store opened in Industry, California, in 1974, because it pioneered an unheard-of concept: the chance to choose from hundreds of different athletic shoes under one roof. Virtually every sport is represented by footwear, and Foot Locker also has its own private-label products. The Foot Locker stores look gritty and industrial, using design materials of raw metal and glass, with TV screens showing sports and music videos.

Lady Foot Locker opened its first store in Joliet, Illinois, in 1982, to address the needs of the dramatically increasing numbers of working women and the women's fitness boom. It remains the only chain committed to offering athletic products specifically for women, and is staffed large-ly by female sales associates. Like its male counterpart, Lady Foot Locker offers its own brand-name products along with a host of others, and a separate website.

Kids Foot Locker, with over 350 stores, is also the preeminent chain in its field of athletic footwear and sports apparel for children. Special attention is paid to monitoring the quick growth of children's feet — associates take part in an extensive fit-training program recognized by the American Podiatric Medical Association. The chain's Double Fit Check Service assures that a second associate checks the fit of each shoe to ensure size and comfort. The stores offer a "buy-10-get-the-11th-free" loyalty card.

*F*oot Locker sells more than just footwear.

*W*ith hundreds of different athletic shoes under one roof, virtually every sport is represented by footwear.

# Gap Inc.

| Parent Company/ Corporate Name: | Gap Inc. |
|---|---|
| Corporate Retail Headquarters: | Two Folsom Street San Francisco, CA 94105, United States 650-952-4400 www.gap.com |
| Annual Revenue: | $16.2 billion (2005) |
| Number of Locations: | 3,000 |
| Countries of Operation: | The U.S., Canada, France, Germany, Japan, the U.K., Singapore and Malaysia |
| Retail Classification: | Specialty |

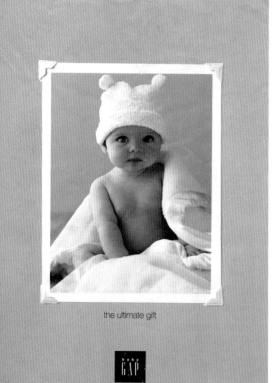

the ultimate gift

*G*ap brands include GapKids, babyGap, GapBody and GapOutlet.

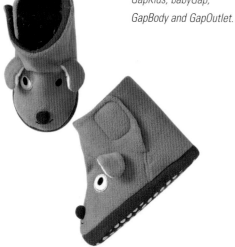

Gap, Banana Republic and Old Navy are among the best-known names in the apparel world, and they all belong to Gap Inc., which has more than 3,000 stores in the U.S., U.K., Canada, France, Japan and Germany.

Its brand names reach men, women, children and babies and also include GapKids, babyGap, GapBody and GapOutlet. Beyond its stores, Gap Inc. also has at least seven sales websites.

Gap and its Gap-related brands provide clothing and accessories that enhance personal style. Banana Republic is famous for casual luxury with high-quality apparel for men and women and sophisticated seasonal collections of accessories, stores, personal care products, intimate apparel and gifts for the home. Old Navy seeks to make "shopping fun again," and is known for its denim, Performance Fleece, graphic T-shirts and cargo jeans.

At product development offices in New York, designers, product managers and graphic artists create the look and feel for each season's merchandise. Resulting products are made in over 50 countries. Each brand has its own marketing team and merchandise is shipped from distribution centers in the U.S., Canada, U.K. and Japan.

The Gap was founded as a single store in San Francisco in 1969, by Donald and Doris Fisher and went public in 1976. In 1983, it bought Banana Republic, then a two-store safari and travel clothing company with a strong catalog business. GapKids started in 1986. The first international Gap store opened the next year in London. In 1990 BabyGap was born, with Old Navy making its debut in 1994.

©*Mark Milian*

©*Mark Milian*

# Guess?, Inc.

| | |
|---|---|
| **Parent Company/ Corporate Name:** | **Guess?, Inc.** |
| Corporate Retail Headquarters: | 1444 S. Alameda Street Los Angeles, CA 90021, United States 213-765-3100 www.guess.com |
| Annual Revenue: | $682 million (2004) |
| Number of Locations: | 444 |
| Countries of Operation: | The U.S., Canada, Australia and other nations in the Americas, Europe, Africa and Asia. |
| Retail Classification: | Apparel |

*Guess? designs, markets and distributes its apparel in stores throughout the U.S., Canada and other nations.*

J

Just a small jeans company at its founding in California in 1981 by two brothers raised in the south of France, Guess? now designs, markets and distributes its full collections of women's and men's apparel in its stores throughout the U.S. and Canada. Its licensed name adorns many product lines around the world.

The brothers, Maurice and Paul Marciano, changed the fashion perception of denim, for which retailers saw little fashion potential in the early 1980s. The Marcianos persuaded a Bloomingdale's store to sell two dozen pairs of its 3-zip Marilyn jeans – the entire stock was sold out within hours. Word spread and the Guess? label was on its way.

As the 1980s progressed, the Guess? product line expanded beyond men's and women's jeans. Soon, baby clothes, watches, footwear, eyewear and perfume bore the licensed Guess? name. In the 1990s, the brand grew internationally and lent its aura to the Guess? Collection, including handbags, activewear, jewelry, swimwear, innerwear, leather, belts, neckwear and men's classic clothing.

*The Guess? collections
include handbags,
activewear, leather
goods and swimwear.*

By 2005, the Guess? wholesale business was found in over 940 U.S. stores. Its retail stores include 157 in the U.S., 51 in Canada and about 236 in other nations from Aruba and Venezuela to Israel and China.

Distinguished as much by its marketing campaigns as by its stylish design, Guess? images have been highly recognizable and regarded in the fashion advertising industry, utilizing many world-famed photographers and an entire generation of supermodels. The company also publishes Guess? Journal, an oversized full color bi-annual magazine.

# H & M
# (Hennes & Mauritz)

| | |
|---|---|
| **Parent Company/ Corporate Name:** | **Hennes & Mauritz AB** |
| Corporate Retail Headquarters: | Norrlandsgatan 15, Box 1421 SE-111 84 Stockholm, Sweden +46-8-796-55-00 www.hm.com |
| Annual Revenue: | $7.2 billion (2004) |
| Number of Locations: | 1,000 |
| Countries of Operation: | 19, including Sweden, Germany, the U.K., Norway, the U.S., the Netherlands, Denmark and throughout Eastern Europe |
| Retail Classification: | Specialty |

Quality fashion at the best price is the philosophy of H&M — Hennes & Mauritz — which owns and solely runs nearly 1,000 stores in 19 countries, selling more than one-half billion items each year.

H&M was established in Sweden in 1947, with the opening of a women's clothing store named Hennes (Swedish for "hers"). It later bought Mauritz Widforss, which offered hunting garb and men's clothing.

Germany is now the chain's biggest market, with 239 stores. Sweden follows with 123, then the U.K. (79), Norway (69), the U.S. (66), The Netherlands (61) and Denmark (53). Other European countries are well represented within the chain, with its newest stores in eastern Europe.

The company specializes in clothing and cosmetics. About 100 designers create its lines, working with 50 pattern designers and about 100 buyers to create its collections for women, men, children and teenagers.

H&M has no factories of its own, but works with about 750 suppliers. About half of its production takes place in Europe, with the rest mainly in Asia.

In the Scandinavian countries, H&M Rowells does a thriving fashion business on the Internet and by mail order. The chain opened several concept lingerie stores in Sweden and the U.K. in 2003 and continues to expand.

*F*ashion is key at H&M.

*A*bout 100 designers create its collections for women, men, children and teenagers.

# The Home Depot, Inc.

**Parent Company/
Corporate Name:** The Home Depot, Inc.

**Corporate Retail
Headquarters:** 2455 Paces Ferry Road, NW
Atlanta, GA 30339-4024, United States
707-433-8211
www.homedepot.com

**Annual Revenue:** $73 billion (2005)

**Number of Locations:** 1,500

**Countries of Operation:** The U.S., Canada, Mexico, China

**Retail Classification:** Specialty

*The opening of the Home Depot's first store in 1979 revolutionized the home improvement industry.*

Building Platforms for Growth

2004 Annual Report

The opening of Home Depot's first store in Atlanta in 1979 revolutionized the home improvement industry. Now, rather than dealing with Main Street hardware stores, do-it-yourselfers could go a warehouse store filled floor to ceiling with virtually any item they would need.

The first stores were attached to Treasure Island outlets and stocked around 25,000 products. Now, the average store in the Home Depot chain of 1,500 outlets carries over 35,000 products and is recognized by its signature "orange box" motif.

Home Depot guarantees low prices on everything it carries. If a customer finds a lower price for a given product at a legitimate, local competitor, Home Depot will beat the price with a 10% discount "to thank you for bringing it to our attention."

Free how-to clinics sponsored by Home Depot are especially popular with the do-it-yourselfers. Home Depot also sponsors Kids Workshops where children accompanied with parents construct projects from prefabricated kits. More than 30 such projects are available, from birdhouses and picture frames to toolboxes and stepstools.

The chain also includes 50 EXPO Design Centers, Home Depot Landscape Supply Centers, APEX Supply and other units. It operates several specialty subsidiaries that specialize in flooring, lighting and plumbing. Home Depot operates in all 50 U.S. states, the District of Columbia, Puerto Rico, eight Canadian provinces and Mexico, and recently opened two sourcing offices in China. All Home Depot stores are company owned and operated; to date, it has never franchised its stores.

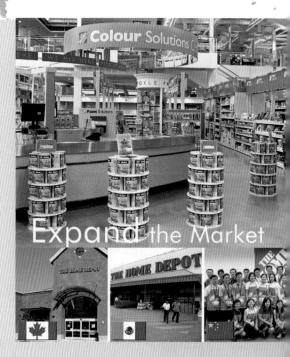

Expand the Market

*H*ome Depot targets do-it-yourselfers with a broad range of products. They also sponsor free how-to clinics.

# Hutchison Whampoa Limited

| | |
|---|---|
| **Parent Company/ Corporate Name:** | Hutchison Whampoa Limited |
| Corporate Retail Headquarters: | Hutchison House, 22nd Floor, 10 Harcourt Road Hong Kong +852-2128-1188 www.hutchison-whampoa.com |
| Annual Revenue: | $17.3 billion (2004) |
| Number of Locations: | 3,700 |
| Countries of Operation: | Hong Kong, China, Taiwan, Singapore, Malaysia, Thailand, and 10 European countries |
| Retail Classification: | Specialty |

*H*utchison Whampoa's A.S. Watson Group operates over 3,700 retail outlets in Asia and Europe.

*F*ocusing on food, health and beauty, and electronics, Watson's stores include PARK n SHOP, Your Personal Store and Fortress.

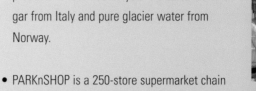

Hutchison Whampoa is a holding company in ports, energy, telecommunications, infrastructure, hotels and property. Its retail division centers on A.S. Watson, one of the best-known trading names in Asia.

Begun as a small dispensary in Guangzhou, China, in 1828, the company moved to Hong Kong in 1841 and became one of the first in the world to produce carbonated soft drinks. By the turn of the century, A.S. Watson had become a major trading force in Hong Kong, the Mainland and in the Philippines.

Today, A.S. Watson Group operates over 3,700 retail outlets in 18 countries in Asia and Europe. The outlets focus on three areas: health and beauty; food, electronics and general merchandise; and manufacturing. Its stores operate under many names:

- Watsons Your Personal Store is the group's original chain of health and beauty products. Its 750 outlets offer a "Look Good. Feel Great. Have Fun" concept and 25,000 different products from more than 20 countries, including cosmetics, personal care items, medicine, health supplements, fashion accessories, confectionery, gifts and toys.

- Great is a luxury supermarket at Pacific Place, where it offers over 20,000 top-of-the-line food products — such as 25-year-old balsamic vinegar from Italy and pure glacier water from Norway.

- PARKnSHOP is a 250-store supermarket chain in Hong Kong, Macau and mainland China.

- Nuance-Watson is the largest retail operator at Hong Kong International Airport, managing 34 world-class duty-free outlets that offer a wide range of goods, including watches and jewelry, fashion and accessories, perfumes, cosmetics, electronic and video equipment, packaged foods and other items.

- Fortress, acquired by Hutchison Whampoa in 1986, is now the leading retailer of electrical appliances in Hong Kong, with over 60 outlets. There are another five outlets in Taiwan.

- Watson's Wine Cellar opened in 1998, offering a larger range of wines than any other wine store in Hong Kong.

*Photos: Courtesy of Hutchison Whampoa Limited*

*W atson's Great store is a luxury supermarket offering over 20,000 top-of-the-line food products.*

# IKEA

| | |
|---|---|
| **Parent Company/ Corporate Name:** | **IKEA International A/S** |
| Corporate Retail Headquarters: | Box 640 SE 25 106 Helsingborg, Sweden +46-42-267-100 www.ikea.com |
| Annual Revenue: | $14.5 billion (2004) |
| Number of Locations: | 152 |
| Countries of Operation: | 22 |
| Retail Classification: | Specialty |

*IKEA developed the concept of flat-packaging that enables customers to assemble products at home.*

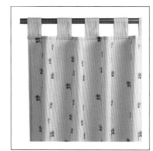

*IKEA offers Scandinavian-style home furnishings and other housewares in their stores throughout the world.*

IKEA is perhaps the world's most widely recognized home furnishings store name, owing to consistency in its bright-yellow-on-bright-blue logo presentation and its Scandinavian-influenced merchandise. Its range of about 10,000 products is consistent in the 152 stores owned and run by the company. There are also about 20 franchised stores throughout the world.

The IKEA idea is to offer a wide range of home furnishings of good design and function at prices low enough that many people can afford them. The company was founded in Sweden in 1943 by Ingvar Kamprad, who took the money awarded him by his father for successfully completing his studies and used it to establish his own business. The name IKEA came from the founder's initials and those of the farm and village where he grew up: Elmtaryd and Agunnaryd.

The first IKEA furniture catalog was published in 1951 and the first showroom opened two years later. In 1955, IKEA began designing its own furniture out of necessity: IKEA's competitors pressured IKEA's suppliers to boycott the new company. Innovation came about in odd ways: One employee needed to remove a table's legs to fit the item into a car, and came up with the idea of knock-down furniture, resulting in IKEA's concept of flat packaging. Another employee thought up IKEA's simple kitchen store ideas while visiting a kitchen manufacturer.

The next 50 years saw a rapid succession of new stores and often new countries being added to the IKEA chain. Many stores now feature playrooms for children and restaurants offering Swedish cuisine. The company also has a healthy mail order business.

Employees' contributions to the chain's growth was so substantial that, in 1999, founder Ingvar Kamprad split an entire day's gross sales equally among the more than 53,000 employees — for many, it was a month's pay from the Big Thank You Event.

*I KEA is one of the worlds most widely recognized names in home furnishings.*

# Inditex   Bershka   **INDITEX**   **Kiddy's Class**   *Massimo Dutti*   oysho

| Parent Company/ Corporate Name: | **Inditex Group** |
|---|---|
| Corporate Retail Headquarters: | Edificio Inditex Avenida de la Diputación 15142 Arteixo, A Coruña, Spain +34-981-18-54-00 www.inditex.com |
| Annual Revenue: | $6.7 billion (2004) |
| Number of Locations: | 2,000 |
| Countries of Operation: | 50 in Europe, the Americas, Asia and Africa |
| Retail Classification: | Specialty |

*Inditex sells clothing on a global scale under such brand names as Zara, Massimo Dutti, Pull and Bear and Stradivarius.*

Inditex is a leading fashion distributors, with eight brand names. The Inditex Group is comprised of over 100 companies in textile design, manufacturing or distribution. The chain dates from the opening of the first Zara store in 1975 in Spain. Portugal followed with its first store in 1988, New York in 1989 and Paris in 1990.

• Inditex's Zara network of 653 stores in 48 countries are located in top locations of major cities. Zara is built on the concept that national borders are no impediment to sharing a single fashion culture.

• Pull and Bear targets urban young people between 14 and 28, incorporating street culture, alternative sports and new technologies in its customer outreach at 354 stores in 17 countries.

- Massimo Dutti presents an independent, urban and cosmopolitan fashion look at its 306 stores in 24 countries. Its clothing uses subtle textures and 100% natural fibers.

- Bershka's 272 stores in 13 countries aim at a younger market for street fashion. The stores are intended as a meeting point for fashion, music and art, with videos, CDs and magazines available for customer entertainment.

- The Stradivarius stores cater to youthful fashion looks through 207 stores in nine countries.

- Oysho offers women's lingerie and undergarments at 86 stores in eight countries.

- Zara Home is the company's home furnishings store, with 41 stores in Spain, Portugal, the U.K. and Greece. Its focus on textiles is complemented by tablewear, cutlery, glassware and linens.

- Kiddy's Class is dedicated to junior fashion, with sections of the 116 stores in Spain and Portugal divided by age to make it easier to find the right outfit, fragrances, cosmetics and accessories.

*The* Zara network of stores can be found in top locations of major cities in 48 countries.

Massimo Dutti | Barcelona | Spain

# Intermarché

| Parent Company/ | |
| --- | --- |
| Corporate Name: | ITM Enterprises SA |

| Corporate Retail Headquarters: | 1 Allée des Mousquetaires, Parc de Tréville |
| --- | --- |
| | F-91078 Bondoufle Cedex, France |
| | +33-1-69-64-10-72 |
| | www.itmentreprises.fr |

| Annual Revenue: | $41.7 billion (2004) |
| --- | --- |
| Countries of Operation: | France, Belgium, Germany, Poland, Portugal, Romania, Spain |
| Retail Classification: | Supermarket, other |

*ITM Enterprises is an association of independent retailers that distributes food products to its 2,900 members in eight European countries.*

ITM Enterprises is an association of independent retailers, called "musketeers." The concern was founded in 1969 by 75 members of the Leclerc cooperative.

ITM is a buying and marketing company that distributes food products to about 2,900 members in eight European countries. France and Germany have the most ITM retail units, which overall number nearly 8,000. Its major supermarket chains are known as Intermarché and Ecomarché.

The rules to become a member of the association are quite strict. Each member may own only three stores, for example, and their size is regulated between about 8,000 and 25,000 square feet.

The group also operates discount stores (called Netto), car accessories stores (Stationmarché), small supermarkets, garden centers (Logimarché), do-it-yourself stores (Bricomarché), textile stores and restaurants (Restaumarché). Some products offered in ITM stores are private label.

*I TM's major supermarket chains are Intermarché and Ecomarché. The group also operates Bricomarché do-it-yourself stores and Restaumarché restaurants.*

# Isetan

## ISETAN

| | |
|---|---|
| **Parent Company/ Corporate Name:** | **Isetan Company Limited** |
| Corporate Retail Headquarters: | 3-14-1 Shinjuku, Shinjuku-ku Tokyo, 160-8011, Japan +81-3-3352-1111 www.isetan.co.jp |
| Annual Revenue: | $5.8 billion (2004) |
| Number of Locations: | 19 |
| Countries of Operation: | Japan, Singapore, China, Malaysia, Austria, Taiwan, Thailand |
| Retail Classification: | Department store |

*I setan department stores sell apparel, housewares, health and beauty products and groceries.*

Isetan operates seven department stores in its homeland of Japan, where it was founded over a century ago. It also has four in Singapore, three in China, two in Malaysia and one each in Austria, Taiwan and Thailand. Its product lines include apparel, health and beauty, housewares, groceries and sundries.

The company also offers its customers financial services, real estate options and travel services. It holds a small part of Barneys New York and also has alliances with the Hankyu and Iwataya department stores in Japan.

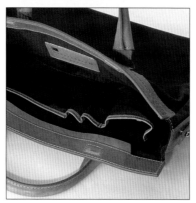

Its company philosophy is expressed as: "We define fashion as fresh new insight, which we can express in every facet of life. We nurture the spirit of fashion that lives in each of us and express it in all that we do. This aesthetic spirit is the breath of fresh air that can add a new sense of excitement to each and every day. Isetan gives new meaning to fashion."

*Founded over a century ago, Isetan operates seven department stores in Japan, as well as stores in Singapore, China, Malaysia and Austria.*

# Ito-Yokado Co., Ltd.

ヨークベニマル

Ito Yokado

| Parent Company/ Corporate Name: | Ito-Yokado Co., Ltd. |
|---|---|
| Corporate Retail Headquarters: | 8-8, Nibancho, Chiyoda-ku Tokyo, 102-8450, Japan 81-3-6238-2111 www.itoyokado.iyg.co.jp |
| Annual Revenue: | $31.9 billion (2004) |
| Number of Locations: | 27,000 |
| Countries of Operation: | Asia, Australia, Europe, North America, South Korea, Taiwan, Thailand |
| Retail Classification: | Convenience store, hypermarket, department store, supermarket |

*The company's participation in 7-Eleven began in 1973, with the signing of a licensing agreement with The Southland Corporation USA.*

*7-Eleven convenience stores, located worldwide, form the foundation of the Ito-Yokado Group.*

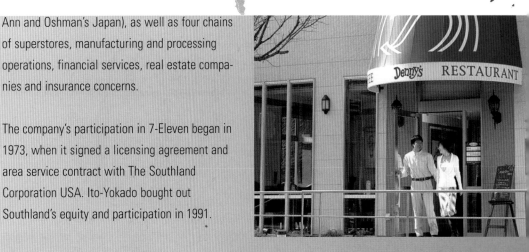

7-Eleven, the worldwide convenience store in 26,850 locations in 18 countries, forms the foundation of Ito-Yokado Group based in Tokyo.

The ubiquitous unit is available for morning coffee, midday snack and the pick-up meal after working late. There are 10,389 7-Elevens in Japan alone. The U.S. makes up the next-largest part of the census, with 5,791 stores, followed by Taiwan (3,625), Thailand (2,590) and South Korea (1,220).

The lucky numbers do not complete the story, however. Ito-Yokado counts 1,300 other stores, including several chains for which it serves as the Japanese franchise. These other components include three supermarket chains (York-Benimaru, York Mart and Sanei), Robinsons department store, three restaurant chains (Denny's Japan, Famil and York Bussan), specialty stores (Mary

Ann and Oshman's Japan), as well as four chains of superstores, manufacturing and processing operations, financial services, real estate companies and insurance concerns.

The company's participation in 7-Eleven began in 1973, when it signed a licensing agreement and area service contract with The Southland Corporation USA. Ito-Yokado bought out Southland's equity and participation in 1991.

*Ito-Yokado serves as the Japanese franchise for Denny's restaurants and Oshman's Sporting Goods stores in Japan.*

# J. Crew

# J. CREW

| | |
|---|---|
| **Parent Company/** **Corporate Name:** | **J. Crew Group, Inc.** |
| Corporate Retail Headquarters: | 770 Broadway New York, New York 10003 (212) 209-2500 www.jcrew.com |
| Annual Revenue: | $804.2 million (2005) |
| Number of Locations: | 245 |
| Countries of Operation: | The U.S., Asia |
| Retail Classification: | Apparel |

©Mark Milian

It all began in 1983 as a collection of sportswear, shoes and accessories featured in lifestyle images on the pages of the J. Crew Outfitters catalog. The company revolutionized casual dress by designing the first stonewashed chinos, the roll-neck sweater and the solid-colored cotton T-shirt with pocket. Expanding on the success of the catalog, the first retail venture premiered in New York City's South Street Seaport in 1989.

Today, J. Crew Group, Inc. is a leading retailer of men's and women's apparel, shoes and accessories, operating retail stores, the J. Crew catalog business, factory-outlet stores and the jcrew.com Web site.

Launched in 1996, jcrew.com, a Web site, allows customers to browse through pages of the catalog and place online orders. J. Crew became one of the first retailers to pioneer the transformation from traditional retailer to the world of e-commerce.

Already an $800 million brand, J. Crew continues to grow rapidly through an expanding retail store network, an industry-leading Web site and a famous catalog as it remains committed to exceeding the expectations of its customers.

*There are about 200 J. Crew retail and factory outlet stores in the U.S. and about 45 outlets in Japan.*

*As a leading retailer of men's and women's apparel, shoes and accessories, J. Crew continues to grow rapidly.*

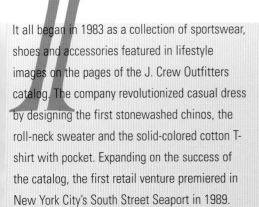

**Women's**
Days off in our summer-weight chinos, linen pullover shirt, and bare-shouldered sundresses.

> J.Crew linen for summer
> See some of your favorites
> View our Women's swim finder
> J.Crew summer staples

# KarstadtQuelle

# KARSTADT QUELLE AG

**Parent Company/ Corporate Name:** **Karstadt Quelle AG**

Corporate Retail Headquarters:
Theodor-Althoff-Strasse 2
D-45133 Essen, Germany
+49-20-17271
www.karstadtquelle.com

Annual Revenue: $16.4 billion (2004)

Number of Locations: 200

Countries of Operation: Germany and other countries in Europe

Retail Classification: Department store, other

*K*arstadt Quelle manages 180 department stores and 305 specialty stores, predominently in Germany.

Karstadt Quelle manages 180 department stores and 305 specialty stores. The company was formed from a merger between the Karstadt department store chain and the leading German mail order group, Quelle. Slightly less than half of its sales comes from over-the-counter retail; slightly less than half from mail order; with the rest coming from its companies in information, financial services and real estate.

Its department stores operate under the names Karstadt (150 locations), Alsterhaus, Hertie, KaDeWe, Quelle and Wertheim. Its mail order brands include Quelle and Neckerman. It also has a 15-store general merchandise chain, Happy Kauf.

Its specialty stores include Golf House, Runners Point and FIFA Shop (sportswear), SinnLeffers (fashion), Schaulandt and WOM (multimedia) and LeBuffet restaurants.

*T*heir specialty stores include the FIFA Shop and Runners Point for sportswear and SinnLeffers for fashion.

# Kesko

# KESKO

**Best** known for its
K-Food store chain,
Kesko is Finland's lead-
ing trading company.

---

| Parent Company/ Corporate Name: | **Kesko** |
|---|---|
| Corporate Retail Headquarters: | Satamakatu 3 FIN-00016 Helsinki, Finland +358-10-5311 www.kesko.fi |
| Annual Revenue: | $7.1 billion (2004) |
| Countries of Operation: | Finland, Estonia, Latvia, Lithuania, Sweden |
| Retail Classification: | Department store, discount, hypermarket, supermarket, food service specialty |

Kesko is Finland's leading trading company. About 53% of its sales comes from its Kesko Food chain, with roughly equal sales from its four other divisions: hardware/builders supplies; agricultural machinery and equipment; home and specialty goods; and cars and international technical trade.

Kesko Food is best known through its K-food store chain. Components include K-citymarkets (low-priced hypermarkets), K-supermarkets (offering food expertise and wide selections of fresh foods), and K-markets (food stores in suburbs and town centers, offering groceries at competitive prices).

The company has its own product brands, the best known of which is Pirkka, comprised of 1,200 Pirkka products.

The Kesko Agro division of Kesko purchases and sells animal feed, chemicals and machinery. The Rautakesko division offers hardware and building supplies. The VV-Auto division imports and markets Volkswagen and Audi cars. The Keswell divi-

sion specializes in the home and specialty goods trade. The Kaukomarkkinat is the leading Finnish trading house operating internationally, with 20 subsidiaries or representative offices abroad. It specializes in technical trading — the import and wholesale of leading branded products and high-quality optics.

Kesko was formed in 1940 through the merger of four regional wholesaling companies that wanted to combine their purchasing power and jointly manage their business operations. The active building of the K-store network soon followed.

*O*ther Kesko divisions include Rautakesko which operates the K-Rauta home improvement chain and KeskoAgro.

*Photos: Courtesy of Kesko*

# Kingfisher

## KING**f**SHER

| Parent Company/ Corporate Name: | Kingfisher |
|---|---|
| Corporate Retail Headquarters: | 3 Sheldon Square Paddington, London W2 6PX, United Kingdom +44-20-7372-8008 www.kingfisher.co.uk |
| Annual Revenue: | $14 billion (2004) |
| Number of Locations: | 569 |
| Countries of Operation: | The U.K., France, Poland, Italy, and other countries in Europe, China, Taiwan |
| Retail Classification: | Specialty |

***K**ingfisher's leading home improvement chain is B & Q. In addition to in-store sales, goods can be ordered from catalogs or on-line.*

Kingfisher is one of Europe's leading home improvement retailers, holding leading market positions in the U.K., France, Poland and Italy, as well as in China and Taiwan. It was known as Woolworth Holdings until 1989.

Its 569 home improvement stores operate in nine countries. Kingfisher also has a strategic alliance with Hornbach, Germany's leading do-it-yourself

retailer, which operates more than 110 stores in Germany and elsewhere in Europe.

Kingfisher's leading home improvement store is B&Q, which has recently introduced new product categories such as bedroom furniture and improved kitchen appliance ranges. It also offers hydrotherapy devices such as saunas and steam cabinets. B&Q has also developed a Special Order brand, through which goods can be ordered in-store, from catalog or online, with delivery to the home.

Its Screwfix Direct is the U.K.'s leading direct supplier of tools and materials for the trade, counting over a million customers.

In France, Kingfisher's operations are known as Castorama (109 stores) and Brico Dépôt (59 stores). B&Q, Castorama and Brico Dépôt are the basis for the company's international activity.

*C*astorama and Brico Depot are popular in France.

# Leroy Merlin

| | |
|---|---|
| **Parent Company/ Corporate Name:** | **The Auchan Group** |
| Corporate Retail Headquarters: | Rue Chanzy – Lezennes 59712 Lille Cedex 9, France +33-03-28-80-80-80 www.leroymerlin.com |
| Annual Revenue: | $7 billion (2004) |
| Number of Locations: | 170 |
| Countries of Operation: | France, Brazil, China, Italy, Portugal, Poland, Russia, Spain |
| Retail Classification: | Specialty |

*Bricocenter in Italy, Aki in Spain and Portugal and Weldom in France are do-it-yourself stores operated by Leroy Merlin.*

Leroy Merlin stores, large do-it-yourself centers averaging 90,000 square feet, are generally located on the outskirts of major towns and cities. Self-service and sales-assisted services are used in the stores. The business centers on five main sectors: do-it-yourself, building, gardening, sanitary equipment and interior decoration.

Customer service helps shoppers prepare their projects, ease the purchase process and partnering in the installation and decoration of their projects. It offers do-it-yourself classes and, in some stores, specialized reading material at book counters.

Leroy Merlin's units are known as Bricocenter in Italy, Aki in Spain and Portugal and Weldom in France. These are generally medium-sized stores providing a large range of self-service sales.

The company was founded in 1923 by Adolphe Leroy and Rose Merlin, who opened a business of American surplus. Strengthened by their early success, they decided to sell do-it-yourself products and supplies at reasonable prices. The name was adopted in 1960 and was unique for its free delivery service. The company is also launching a store in Greece.

*In* addition to do-it-yourself products, stores also offer building materials, gardening supplies and decorative items.

# Lidl

| | |
|---|---|
| **Parent Company/ Corporate Name:** | **The Schwarz Group** |
| Corporate Retail Headquarters: | Sekretariat Immobilien, Rötelstraße 30 74166 Neckarsulm, Germany +49-7132-30-6060 www.lidl.de |
| Annual Revenue: | $42.8 billion (2004) |
| Number of Locations: | 5,600 |
| Countries of Operation: | Germany, Denmark, Hungary, Norway, Slovenia, France, Austria, Belgium, the Czech Republic, Finland, France, Ireland, Italy, Spain, Sweden, the U.K |
| Retail Classification: | Supermarket, hypermarket, discount, department store |

*A*s a major European food dealer, Lidl offers over 1,200 different products under their own brand name.

*G*erman discounter Lidl operates about 5,000 deep discount stores and supermarkets and sells everything from produce to PCs.

There's nothing little about Lidl & Schwarz. The German discounter sells everything from purses and peas to produce and PCs. Lidl operates about 5,000 deep discount department stores and no-frills Lidl supermarkets throughout Europe (about 2,000 in Germany), making it one of Germany's largest grocery chains. The stores commonly carry about 800 different items, mostly under Lidl's own brand. Lidl isn't idle either, as it's expanding into Denmark, Hungary, Norway and Slovenia. By emulating ALDI's low-cost operating methods, Lidl is challenging and even outpacing its rival in some markets, notably France. Billionaire Dieter Schwarz and family control Lidl.

Lidl's history goes back to the 1930s, when Lidl & Schwarz Grocery Wholesale was founded in Germany. Since then Lidl has diversified into hypermarkets under the trading name "Kaufland" and discount food stores known as "Lidl". Today, the Schwarz Group is one of the largest grocery retailers in Europe with over 5,600 stores and includes the following: Kaufland – large super-markets/hypermarkets; Handelshof, Concord – supermarkets; Lidl – discount supermarkets; and Ruef – wholesale markets.

The first Lidl stores were opened in 1973 and by the 1980s Lidl was a household name throughout Germany. During the 1990s Lidl started to open stores outside Germany and today Lidl stores can be found in nearly every country in Europe includ-ing Germany, Austria, Belgium, Czech Republic,

Finland, France, Ireland, Italy, Norway, Spain, Sweden and the U.K. Lidl is now well established as a major European food retailer offering over 1,200 different products -- mostly under Lidl's own brand.

*O utside Germany, Lidl stores can be found in nearly every country in Europe including France, Italy, Sweden and the U.K.*

# LVMH

## LVMH
### MOËT HENNESSY . LOUIS VUITTON

| Parent Company/ Corporate Name: | LVMH |
|---|---|
| Corporate Retail Headquarters: | 22, avenue Montaigne 75008 Paris, France +33-1-44-13-22-22 www.lvmh.com |
| Annual Revenue: | $4.2 billion (2004) |
| Number of Locations: | 1,500 |
| Countries of Operation: | Worldwide |
| Retail Classification: | Department store, supermarket, specialty |

©DFS

*L* VMH offers the top name brands in wines and spirits, fashion and leather goods and jewelry and perfume.

©Mark Milian

*T*he company's retail divisions include Sephora cosmetic stores (pictured left in a California location), Le Bon Marche and La Samaritaine department stores and Miami Cruiseline duty-free shops.

©Lvan Lamsweerde & V. Matadin/Givenchy

©Loewe

©TAG Heuer

©P. Demarchelier

©*Miami Cruiseline Services*

LVMH is Moët Hennessy-Louis Vuitton, a group specializing in luxury. Its 50 brands, organized into five sectors, are the top names in luxury goods:

- Its Wines & Spirits sector includes Moët & Chandon, Dom Pérignon and Krug Champagnes; Château d'Yquem; wine and Hennessy cognac.

- Fashion & Leather Goods list such well-known names as Louis Vuitton, Loewe, Celine, Berluti, Givenchy, Fendi and Donna Karan International.

- Perfumes & Cosmetics offer Christian Dior, Guerlain and Givenchy.

- Watches & Jewelry include TAG Heuer, Zenith and Dior Watches, among others.

- Selective Retailing focuses on DFS Group (a retailer for international travelers), Miami Cruiseline (duty-free shops), Sephora (beauty and skin care), Le Bon Marché (department stores, food stores and real estate) and La Samaritaine (department store).

©*Mark Milian (above and below)*

©*Tzu-Chen Chen*

©*Moët & Chandon*

©*Nick Knight*

**W**ines and spirits include Dom Perignon and Moët & Chandon. Their watches and jewelry include TAG Heuer and Dior.

# Marks & Spencer

| | |
|---|---|
| **Parent Company/ Corporate Name:** | **Marks & Spencer** |
| Corporate Retail Headquarters: | 47-67 Baker Street, Michael House London W1A 1DN, United Kingdom +44-20-7935-4422 www.marksandspencer.co.uk |
| Annual Revenue: | $14.2 billion (2004) |
| Number of Locations: | 550 |
| Countries of Operation: | England and 27 others in Asia, the Americas and Europe |
| Retail Classification: | Department store, supermarket |

*S*ome 10 million people shop for clothing, food and housewares in Marks & Spencer's 375 U.K. stores each week.

*Photos: Courtesy of Marks & Spencer*

Marks & Spencer is one of the U.K.'s leading retailers of food, clothes, food, home products and financial services. Some 10 million people shop in its 375 U.K. stores each week.

There are also 155 stores managed under franchise in 27 other countries. In Asia, the largest numbers are in Hong Kong, Indonesia and Thailand (10 stores each), the Philippines (11 stores), South Korea (12 stores) and Turkey (15 stores). In Europe, the largest clusters are in Greece (17), Cyprus (8), Finland (6), and Ireland (7). The U.S. has 27 Kings Super Markets owned by Marks & Spencer.

The department stores sell reasonably priced clothing, food and housewares through the company's house label St. Michael.

Its lineage dates back to 1884 and a stall leased by Russian-born Polish refugee Michael Marks, who 10 years later partnered with Tom Spencer, a wholesale company cashier. Marks' son, Simon, became company chairman in 1916 after the founders' deaths. In the 1920s, the company took the unprecedented step of starting to buy

directly from manufacturers. In 1928, the St. Michael trade mark was registered and in November 1930, the company's flagship store was opened at Marble Arch, London.

Food stores and Café Bars were added in the 1930. A self-service trial in one store proved successful and was rolled out elsewhere. In 1975, the first stores opened in continental Europe.

*M*arks & Spencer stores can be found in Europe, Asia and the Americas. They also own Kings Supermarkets in the U.S.

# McDonald's Corporation

| | |
|---|---|
| **Parent Company/**<br>**Corporate Name:** | McDonald's |
| Corporate Retail | McDonald's Plaza<br>Oak Brook, IL 60523, United States<br>630-623-3000<br>www.mcdonalds.com |
| Annual Revenue: | $20.5 billion (2005) |
| Number of Locations: | 30,000 |
| Countries of Operation: | 119 |
| Retail Classification: | Food service |

*With over 30,000 restaurants in 119 countries, McDonald's serves food to over 47 million people daily.*

McDonald's has more than 30,000 restaurants in 119 countries. Quarter Pounders, Chicken McNuggets, Egg McMuffins and other McDonald's branded foods are consumed by over 47 million people each day.

McDonald's also holds a substantial market share in each nation where it is located. From Canada to Croatia, from India to Israel, McDonald's is recognized by its famous "golden arches" and its attentiveness to customer service. The menu is sometimes modified to reflect local custom and culture.

Speed of service is increased by the chain's long-standing drive-in windows and the continual elimination of slow-selling items or food sizes.

The McDonald's success story began in 1954, when Ray Kroc mortgaged his home and invested his life savings to become the exclusive distributor of a fine-spindled milk shake maker called the Multimixer. He visited California restaurateurs Dick and Mac McDonald and was amazed to see the speed of service to hamburger-hungry customers. He went there hoping to convince the McDonalds to open up several new stores, intent on selling eight Multimixers to each. On their suggestion that he run restaurants instead, Kroc returned to Des Plaines, Illinois, where the first McDonald's opened in 1955 with first-day revenues of $366.12. Now, gross sales top $20 billion.

Since those early days, McDonald's has grown to its powerful international presence, as demonstrated by its first store in Kuwait City in 1994, where 15,000 patient customers queued up and the line for the drive-up window was seven miles long.

*"Ronald McDonald" became the company's spokesclown in 1963. Ronald McDonald House has given over $400 million in grants to benefit children.*

"Ronald McDonald" became the company's spokesclown in 1963, and the Ronald McDonald House Charities have given away $400 million in grants to benefit children. McDonald's owns the Boston Market and Chipotle Mexican Grill casual restaurant chains.

*McDonald's also owns the Boston Market and Chipotle Mexican Grill restaurant chains.*

# METRO Group

## METRO Group

### The Spirit of Commerce

| | |
|---|---|
| **Parent Company/ Corporate Name:** | **METRO AG** |
| Corporate Retail Headquarters: | Schlüterstrasse 1 40235 Düsseldorf, Germany +49-211-6886-2217 www.metrogroup.de |
| Annual Revenue: | $69.8 billion (2004) |
| Number of Locations: | 1,435 |
| Countries of Operation: | 28, in Europe, Asia and Africa |
| Retail Classification: | Hypermarket, supermarket, department store, specialty |

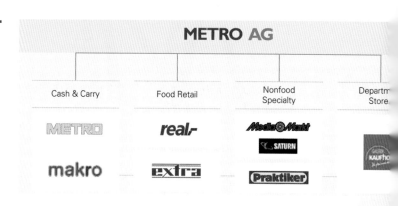

| METRO AG | | | |
|---|---|---|---|
| Cash & Carry | Food Retail | Nonfood Specialty | Departm... Store... |
| METRO | real,- | Media Markt SATURN | GALERIA KAUFHOF |
| makro | extra | Praktiker | |

*M*ETRO Group owns and operates 130 Kaufhof department stores and 290 Real hypermarkets.

# M

METRO Group is a leading trading and retailing group in Europe and the world, with a presence in 28 countries. Almost half of its sales are in non–German stores.

While threads of the company's development can be traced back to 1880, the Metro company itself dates from 1964, when Otto Beisheim opened the first Metro Cash & Carry store, a wholesale market where traders could collect their merchandise against cash. METRO AG itself was formed in 1996, with the merger of several independent retail companies.

METRO serves as a holding company for six sales divisions:

- Metro Cash & Carry and Makro brand names comprise the wholesale division, which accounts for about 46% of the company's sales. Worldwide, these 477 stores offer about 20,000 food items and 30,000 nonfood products for purchase by retailers.

- METRO's 290 Real hypermarkets offer a broad range of food and nonfood products in an average selling space of 50,000 to 80,000 square feet. Metro estimates that over one million customers shop there every day, with another half-million shopping at least once weekly.

Germany hosts 256 Real hypermarkets, with 34 elsewhere. METRO now includes 85 former Wal-Mart stores.

- Extra is a leading supermarket chain in Germany. Food accounts for over 90% of sales. Extra's private label "Tip" has a strong consumer following.

- Praktiker is METRO's home improvement division, with a total of 338 stores, with 282 in Germany. Products include building, gardening and decorating.

- Media products are the main draw for two store chains. Media Markt is a leading European marketer of consumer electronics, with about 180 stores in Germany. Saturn stores offer CDs, sound media, telecommunications, computer and photography products.

- Kaufhof department stores number 130 in 80 German cities, usually in downtowns. This division also includes 15 stores in the Belgian department store chain Inno.

*O*ther METRO banners include Praktiker home improvement chain, Media Markt consumer electronics chain and Extra supermarkets.

# Mitsukoshi, Ltd.

## MITSUKOSHI

| | |
|---|---|
| **Parent Company/ Corporate Name:** | **Mitsui Group** |
| Corporate Retail Headquarters: | 1-4-1 Nihonbashi Muromachi, Chuo-ku Tokyo, 103-8001, Japan +81-3-3241-3311 www.mitsukoshi.co.jp |
| Annual Revenue: | $7.9 billion (2004) |
| Number of Locations: | 102 |
| Countries of Operation: | Japan, the U.S., China, France, Italy, Spain, the U.K., Germany |
| Retail Classification: | Department store |

*As a creative retailer, Mitsukoshi provides innovative merchandise and superior service to its customers.*

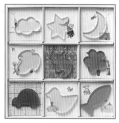     

   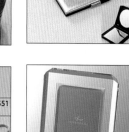  

Mitsukoshi, one of Japan's leading department store chains, was founded as a single kimono shop in 1673. In Japan, the retailer runs more than 10 domestic main stores, about 80 smaller stores, and another dozen outlets in other countries, including the U.S., China, France, Italy, Spain, the U.K. and Germany.

Mitsukoshi group continuously aims to be a creative retailer that always provides innovative merchandise and superior service to customers with traditional principles of "The spirit of sincerity" and "Always together with the customer." Rich in history, Mitsukoshi has always strived to retain architectural distinction in its store designs, in some instances incorporating decorative gardens, artistic lighting, and impressive monuments. Always innovative, however, Mitsukoshi has plans to open stores in shopping centers with the goal of reaching the younger consumer.

*There are 10 main stores in Japan and another dozen outlets in other countries including the U.S., China, France and Spain.*

*In order to reach the younger consumer, Mitsukoshi plans to open its stores in shopping centers.*

写真は税込3,150円の商品です。

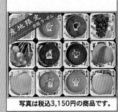

写真は税込3,150円の商品です。

Bridal Index
Tangerine

MITSUKOSHI

# Office Depot

| | |
|---|---|
| **Parent Company/ Corporate Name:** | **Office Depot, Inc.** |
| Corporate Retail | 2200 Old Germantown Road Delray Beach, FL 33445, United States 561-438-4800 www.officedepot.com |
| Annual Revenue: | $9.5 billion (2004) |
| Number of Locations: | 1,047 |
| Countries of Operation: | The U.S., Australia, Canada, Colombia, Costa Rica, Guatemala, Israel, Japan, Mexico, Thailand, 13 European countries |
| Retail Classification: | Specialty |

*Office Depot sells office products at 1,000 company-owned and licensed stores world- wide, as well as through its catalogs and internet sites.*

*In addition to office supplies, stores offer computer equipment, office furniture, school supplies and printing and copying services.*

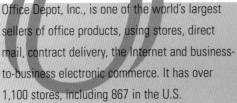

Office Depot, Inc., is one of the world's largest sellers of office products, using stores, direct mail, contract delivery, the Internet and business-to-business electronic commerce. It has over 1,100 stores, including 867 in the U.S.

Its first store opened in 1986 in Fort Lauderdale, Florida. Copy and printing services were introduced two years later. The company experienced rapid growth during the late 1980s, expanding to 173 stores in 27 states by the close of 1990. Under the company's Viking brand, it opened its first distribution center in the U.K. that year. A series of acquisitions took place in the early 1990s. During that decade, operations blossomed in Australia, Israel, Colombia, Poland, Mexico, Germany, The Netherlands, Ireland, France, Hungary, Thailand, Austria, Japan and Italy.

The company's public website opened in 1998, with e-commerce sites operating under the Office Depot or Viking names launched for several European countries in 2000. In 2003 the company launched a new Spanish–language website (www.espanol.officedepot.com), noting that it "marks the first fully-functional Spanish language web site in the office supply retail industry." There are now 34 international websites.

Office Depot also operates a website exclusively for teachers and students to purchase school supplies (www.school.com).

*Countries of operation include France, the U.K., Mexico, Australia and Japan. Office Depot also sells through 34 international websites.*

# OfficeMax

**OfficeMax**
What's your thing?™

| | |
|---|---|
| Parent Company/ Corporate Name: | OfficeMax, Inc. |
| Corporate Retail Headquarters: | 150 E. Pierce Road Itasca, IL 60143, United States 630-438-7800 www.officemax.com |
| Annual Revenue: | $6.7 billion (2004) |
| Number of Locations: | 1,000 |
| Countries of Operation: | The U.S., Canada, Mexico |
| Retail Classification: | Specialty |

*In addition to business supplies, office furniture and a wide range of technology products, OfficeMax also provides printing services.*

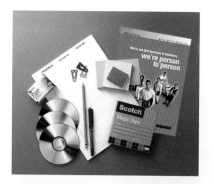

*OfficeMax offers thousands of name-brand and OfficeMax branded products through stores, direct mail and internet websites.*

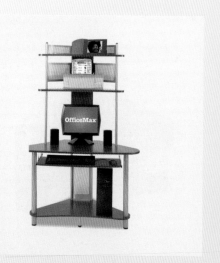

OfficeMax is a chain of office supply superstores that quickly grew organically and through acquisitions until it was bought by Boise Office Solutions in 2003.

Cleveland, Ohio, was the site of the first OfficeMax store, opening in July 1988. Michael Feuer and seven associates established the company, which by year's end had opened a total of three superstores. By the close of 1989, the number had risen to 11 superstores in four states.

The 1990s saw the greatest acquisition activity, with purchases of seven Office World stores, five Kmart Office Square Superstores, 41 OW Office Warehouse stores and 1-5 BizMart stores. Going public in 1994, the company also introduced its first FurnitureMax store-within-a-store module that year.

E-commerce began in 1995, and in 1996 the company surpassed 500 stores. Its first store opened in Mexico that year.

By 1997 the company exceeded $3 billion in annual sales, which OfficeMax says is only the fourth company in U.S. history to do so in less than nine years. An agreement with Hewlett Packard in 2001 led to selling computers and accessories in OfficeMax stores. By 2002, there were 30 OfficeMax locations in Mexico, with online and direct mail operations in Canada as well.

The acquisition by Boise Office Products in 2003 expanded the joint companies' outreach under the name OfficeMax.

# Otto's

## otto group

| Parent Company/ Corporate Name: | Otto GmbH & Co. KG |
|---|---|
| Corporate Retail Headquarters: | Wandsbeker Strasse 3-7 2217 Hamburg, Germany +49-40-64-61-0 www.ottogroup.com |
| Annual Revenue: | $12 billion (2004) |
| Number of Locations: | About 70 |
| Countries of Operation: | 19 |
| Retail Classification: | Specialty |

*O tto's best-known retail group is the Crate & Barrel chain, which offers home furnishings, housewares and accessories through 128 stores in the U.S.*

*Above and below: Courtesy of the Otto Group*

The Otto Group is a leading internationally active trading and services group, comprised of about 123 companies in 19 countries. It was founded in 1949 as the Otto Versand shoe store. Its first catalog offered 28 pairs of shoes on 14 pages. Currently, Otto has 62 catalogs with a total circulation of 109 million copies, offering about 130,000 items.

Today, Otto has separate units for retail sales, financial services, wholesale trading and other services, which are coordinated in the interests of better customer service.

The retail trade group operates in Europe, North America and Asia. Its core business is mail-order, complemented by retail store sales and e-commerce. It is exploring TV shopping as yet another means to engage customers. It operates about 70 general merchandise stores in Switzerland. Retailing accounts for most of the company's total sales.

*O ther companies in the Otto Group include Fegro/Selgros, a cash-and-carry supplier and the Actebis Group, which focuses on information technology.*

One of Otto's best-known retail groups is Crate and Barrel, founded in Chicago in a closed-down elevator factory in 1962 and acquired by the Otto Group in 1998. There are now 128 Crate and Barrel stores, providing household goods, furniture and living accessories from many countries for U.S. customers.

A few of the other companies under the Otto Group umbrella are 3 Suisses International Group, which specializes in the distance selling of products and services to consumers and businesses; Otto Freizeit und Touristik GmbH, which offers tourism-related services through its Otto Reisen concern; Actebis Group, which focuses on information technology; and Fegro/Selgros, a cash-and-carry supplier.

# Payless ShoeSource, Inc.

| | |
|---|---|
| **Parent Company/ Corporate Name:** | Payless ShoeSourse, Inc. |
| Corporate Retail Headquarters: | 3231 SE 6th Avenue Topeka, KS 66607, United States 877-452-7500 www.payless.com |
| Annual Revenue: | $2.7 billion (2005) |
| Number of Locations: | 5,000 |
| Countries of Operation: | The Americas |
| Retail Classification: | Specialty |

Payless ShoeSource, Inc., is a major family footwear retailer in the Western Hemisphere. The company sells more than 200 million pairs of shoes annually.

Payless was founded in 1956 by two cousins who developed a new idea: selling shoes in a self-service environment, freeing customers from waiting for salesclerks.

Its 5,000 stores are located in all 50 U.S. states, plus Puerto Rico, Guam, Saipan, the U.S. Virgin Islands, Canada, Central America, the Caribbean and South America. Stores feature affordable, fashionable, quality footwear for women, men and children, sold in a self-selection format. Most shoes sell for less than $15 every day, and frequent sales and promotions reduce prices further. The broad assortment of footwear includes basic, seasonal and fashion shoes in dress, casual, athletic, work boot and specialty categories.

Stores are located in a variety of settings, from urban to rural, including regional malls, strip centers, central business districts and free-standing buildings. Payless also has sales locations in other retailers' stores through its ShopKo® store-within-a-store strategy.

*W*ith 5,000 stores, Payless ShoeSource can be found in neighborhood and community centers, malls and freestanding buildings.

*P*ayless stores feature affordable, fashionable, quality footwear for women, men and children, sold in a self-service environment.

# Pick'n Pay

![Pick'n Pay logo]

| | |
|---|---|
| **Parent Company/ Corporate Name:** | **Pick'n Pay Retailers (Pty) Ltd** |
| Corporate Retail Headquarters: | Corner of Main & Campground Roads, Claremont Cape Town 7708, South Africa +27-21-6581000 www.pnp.co.za |
| Annual Revenue: | $5 billion (2004) |
| Number of Locations: | 667 |
| Countries of Operation: | South Africa, Australia and four other African countries |
| Retail Classification: | Supermarket, hypermarket |

The Pick'n Pay Group in South Africa is one of Africa's largest and most consistently successful retailers of food, clothing and general merchandise. Founded in 1967, it now operates through three divisions:

- The Retail Division manages Pick'n Pay branded businesses, including 14 hypermarkets, 175 supermarkets, family franchises, minimarket franchises and home shopping. The supermarkets have three in-house product brands: No Name, Pick'n Pay's Choice and Foodhall.

- The Group Enterprises Division operate the brands other than Pick'n Pay, which include Score Supermarkets, TM Supermarkets, Property and Go Banking. This division also seeks out new investment opportunities for the group.

*The company aims to achieve "a climate of dignity, respect and freedom" among its employees towards its customers.*

- The Australia Division manages 77 Franklin supermarkets in New South Wales. It recently embarked on developing its own food distribution channels (separate from its distribution arrangement with Metcash) and sees future growth coming from franchising.

Social conduct plays a large role in Pick'n Pay's outreach to the public. It aims to achieve "a climate of dignity, respect and freedom" among its employees toward its customers. "Living in the current South African environment, it is too easy to dwell on the negativity which faces us on a day-to-day basis," says the company's website. "We should not lose sight of all the miraculous strides that have been made both in South African society at large and within our Company."

*Pick 'n Pay in South Africa is one of the largest and most successful retailers of food, clothing and general merchandise in Africa.*

# PPR Group (Pinault-Printemps-Redoute)

| **Parent Company/ Corporate Name:** | **PPR SA** |
|---|---|
| Corporate Retail Headquarters: | 10, Avenue Hoche<br>75381 Paris Cedex 08, France<br>+33-1-45-64-61-00<br>www.pprgroup.com |
| Annual Revenue: | $15.7 billion (2004) |
| Countries of Operation: | France, the U.S., Taiwan, Brazil and 11 other European countries |
| Retail Classification: | Specialty |

©Richard Burbridge

| DISTRIBUTION | LUXE |
|---|---|
| PRINTEMPS | GUCCI |
| REDCATS | Yves Saint Laurent |
|  | BOTTEGA VENETA |
| fnac.com | YSL BEAUTE |
|  | B BOUCHERON PARIS |
| Conforama | BEDAT & C° GENEVE |
|  | BALENCIAGA |
| CFAO | sergio rossi |
|  | STELLA McCARTNEY |
|  | ALEXANDER McQUEEN |

*P*PR luxury brands include Yves St. Laurent, Bottega Veneta, Sergio Rossi, Bedat & Co., and Boucheron.

GUCCI
ENVY
me

The New Fragrance for Women

*P*PR has had an increasing interest in the Gucci luxury line.

Pinault-Printemps-Redoute (PPR) is one of Europe's largest companies in specialized distribution and among the largest luxury goods groups in the world. It grew from the Pinault Group, founded in 1963 to do timber trading.

In the 1990s, PPR acquired an eclectic range of companies: a pharmaceutical distributor, a women's lingerie chain, a home shopping company, an office supply and equipment firm, an electrical equipment distributor, a retailer and a mail-order company.

In 1999, PPR bought 44% of the Gucci Group. Later, Gucci bought Yves Saint Laurent, YSL Beauté, Sergio Rossi, Boucheron, Bédat & Co., Bottega Veneta and Balenciaga. The strengthening of Gucci/PPR's brand line persuaded PPR to concentrate its business on retail and luxury goods and in 2002 PPR increased its stake in Gucci.

Other retailing activity includes stores selling fashion, beauty, home furnishings, books, digital entertainment and consumer electronics through such brands as Conforama, Fnac, Mobile Planet, Printemps, Redcats, Orcanta, Kadéos and CFAO.

*O*ther PPR retailers include Printemps (department stores), Conforama (home furnishings and consumer electronics) and Redcats (catalog and internet shopping).

# Reitan Group

Lade Gaard

| | |
|---|---|
| **Parent Company/ Corporate Name:** | **Reitan Group** |
| Corporate Retail Headquarters: | Uranienborgveien 6<br>Oslo 0308, Norway<br>+47-22-43-31-00<br>www.reitanhandel.no |
| Annual Revenue: | $4.2 billion (2004) |
| Number of Locations: | 1,900 |
| Countries of Operation: | Denmark, Estonia, Latvia, Lithuania, Norway, Slovak Republic, Sweden |
| Retail Classification: | Supermarket, convenience store, discount, food service, specialty |

The Reitan Group is a franchise-based retail company. With its affiliates, it operates 1,900 sales points in several northern European countries.

Reitan's corporate strategy is "three concepts in three countries" — the grocery store chain REMA 1000, the "kiosk chain" Narvesen/Pressbyrån and the convenience store chain 7-Eleven — in Norway, Sweden and Denmark. Those countries account for about 1,400 of Reitan's stores. The company also has a substantial property portfolio.

Reitan owns 100% of the 7-Eleven Chain in those countries, as well as 100% of the REMA 1000 International's 512 stores in those countries plus Slovakia.

The Narvesen/Pressbyrån chain is comprised of nearly 1,200 convenience stores in Norway, Sweden and Latvia, and it holds a dominant market position in each. Reitan owns 100% of the Norway (Narvesen) and Sweden (Pressbyrån) operations. The Finnish–owned company Finske Rautakirja and Reitan each own 50% of the Latvian chain, which is called Preses Apvieniba.

Reitan's origins were at Ole Reitan's Grocery Store, which opened in 1948 in Trondheim, Norway. Other groceries were opened throughout the 1960s and 1970s. By 1990 Reitan had reached its goal of being present in every Norwegian city and town with a population of 10,000 or more.

*T*he Reitan Group operates the REMA 1000 grocery chain, the Narvesen/Pressbyran "kiosk chain" and the 7-Eleven convenience store chain in Norway, Sweden and Denmark.

# REWE Handelsgruppe

| | |
|---|---|
| **Parent Company/ Corporate Name:** | REWE Handelsgruppe/AG |
| Corporate Retail Headquarters: | Domstrasse 20 Cologne 50668, Germany +49-221-149-0 www.rewe.de |
| Annual Revenue: | $42.8 billion (2004) |
| Number of Locations: | 11,196 |
| Countries of Operation: | Germany and 12 other European countries |
| Retail Classification: | Supermarket, hypermarket, drug store, specialty |

*R*ewe banners include Rewe-Der-Supermarkt and Rewe-Nahkauf, Billa and Penny Market. The toom do-it-yourself stores offer home improvement products.

*R*ewe Zentral operates about 11,000 stores in Europe. Food retail stores account for most of Rewe's sales.

REWE-Zentral AG owns 8,560 stores in Germany and about 2,600 elsewhere in Europe. It also owns the cooperative Rewe Trading Group.

Food retail stores account for about 82% of Rewe's sales. Independent Rewe retailers operate stores primarily under the brands Rewe-Der Supermarkt and Rewe-Nahkauf. Other major retailer grocery brands include Billa, Pick Pay and visavis. Rewe also has affiliate enterprises such as HL, MiniMal, Penny Market and the cash-and-carry stores Fegros/Sellgros and Handelshof.

Beyond food, Rewe runs about 1,000 specialty stores. Idea drugstores ("the green chemist store") feature chemist products, skincare items and cosmetics. The 243 toom do-it-yourself stores offer building, renovation and interior decoration products, and many incorporate modern garden centers. Rewe's ProMarkt stores sell entertainment electronics, household appliances, PC hardware and software and a wide range of telecommunications products.

Rewe also has a tourism division (Rewe Touristik) comprised of 1,100 travel agencies and eight tour-operation companies.

# Royal Ahold

**㊉ Ahold**

| | |
|---|---|
| **Parent Company/ Corporate Name:** | Royal Ahold |
| **Corporate Retail Headquarters:** | Albert Heijnweg 1 <br> 1507 EH Zaandam, The Netherlands <br> +31-0-75-659-9111 <br> www.ahold.com |
| **Annual Revenue:** | $44.8 billion (2004) |
| **Number of Locations:** | 8,500 |
| **Countries of Operation:** | The Netherlands, the U.S., Spain, Portugal, the Czech Republic, Slovakia, Belgium, Poland, Sweden, Norway, Denmark, Latvia, Lithuania, Estonia |
| **Retail Classification:** | Supermarkets, hypermarkets, convenience stores, and other formats |

*O*perating almost 7,000 stores in Europe and over 1,600 stores in the U.S., Royal Ahold is one of the largest international food retailers.

Royal Ahold is a holding company and one of the largest international food retailers, with supermarket chains throughout the U.S. and Europe.

The company started in 1887, when 22-year-old Alber Heijn took over his father's small grocery store near Zaandam, West Holland. His focus on quality products and services at the lowest prices continues to inform the policies of Royal Ahold today. It serves the needs of over 40 million customers each week.

In the U.S. it operates over 1,600 stores, largely along the eastern seaboard, under the names Stop & Shop, Giant-Landover, Giant-Carlisle, BI-LO, Tops, and Bruno's. U.S. Foodservice is a wholly owned subsidiary of Royal Ahold, providing food and related products to its customer base of over 300,000 institutional and food service establishments, including hotels, health care institutions, government facilities, universities, sports stadiums, and caterers. Royal Ahold also operates Peapod, the leading internet e-grocer in the U.S.

In Europe, Royal Ahold operates almost 7,000 stores in 13 countries. About one-third are in The Netherlands, including its flagship supermarket company Albert Heijn. Royal Ahold has a joint venture in Northern Europe through which it operates the ICA Group, Scandinavia's largest food retailer, with nearly 3,000 stores. In Portugal it co-owns the supermarket chain Pingo Doce and the Feira Nova hypermarkets. In The Czech Republic it operates over 200 stores, including the Albert supermarket chain and the Hypernova hypermarkets. Its Deli XL food service distribution unit provides food and nonfood products to hospitals, schools and other hospitality enterprises in The Netherlands.

Royal Ahold also owns several smaller store chains in The Netherlands: Gall & Gall liquor stores, Etos health and beauty care stores, Jamin confectionary stores, De Tuinen (natural products) and Ter Huurne, whose stores are on the Dutch–German border.

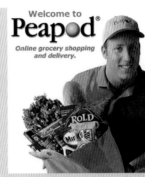

*S*erving 40 million customers each week, Royal Ahold focuses on quality products and services. The company also operates Peapod, the leading internet e-grocer in the U.S.

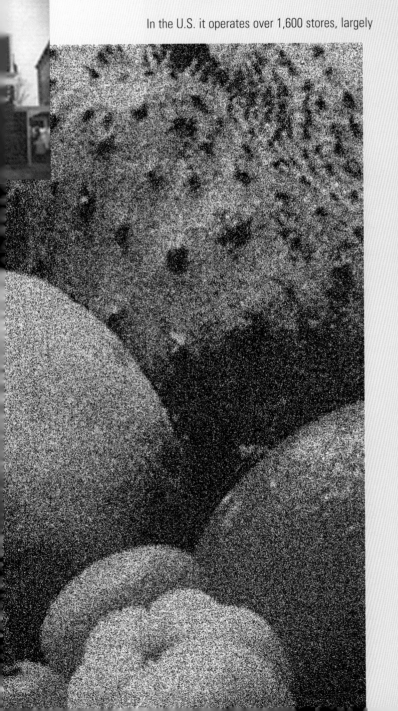

# Safeway

# SAFEWAY Ⓢ
## Ingredients for life.™

| Parent Company/ Corporate Name: | Safeway |
|---|---|
| Corporate Retail Headquarters: | 5918 Stoneridge Mall Road Pleasanton, CA 94588-3229 United States 925-467-3000 www.safeway.com |
| Annual Revenue: | $35.8 billion (2004) |
| Number of Locations: | 1,817 |
| Countries of Operation: | U.S., Canada, Mexico |
| Retail Classification: | Supermarket |

*Safeway's 1,800 stores operate under a variety of names including Safeway, Vons and Dominick's in the U.S., Safeway in Canada and Casa Ley in Mexico.*

Safeway operates 1,817 food store and drug-stores in the western and Mid-Atlantic regions of the U.S., and in western Canada. The company also holds an interest in Casa Ley, S.A. de C.V., which operates 108 food and general merchandise stores in western Mexico.

The stores operate under a variety of names: Safeway (1,137 stores in the U.S. and Canada), Vons and Vons Food and Drug (325), Dominick's (113), Casa Ley (99, in Mexico), Tom Thumb (70, in Texas), Randall's (67, in Texas), Genuardi's (38, in the Philadelphia area), Pavilions (32), Carr's (17, in Alaska), Pak 'n Save (12), Eagle (7), and Simon David (1).

A majority of the stores also have specialty departments: bakeries (94%), floral (92%) and pharmacy (74%).

Safeway has one of the largest private label programs in North America. Customers can choose from 2,500 products named Safeway, Lucerne and Mrs. Wright's. An additional 1,250 premium products are marketed under the Safeway SELECT label.

The company also has an extensive network of distribution, manufacturing and food processing facilities. This network includes nine milk plants, eight bread-making plants and others for ice cream, cheese/meat, soft drinks, fruits/vegetables and pet foods.

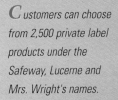

*C*ustomers can choose from 2,500 private label products under the Safeway, Lucerne and Mrs. Wright's names.

# Schlecker

# SCHLECKER

| | |
|---|---|
| **Parent Company/ Corporate Name:** | **Fa. Anton Schlecker** |
| Corporate Retail Headquarters: | Talstrasse 12 D-89579 Ehingen, Germany +49-73-91-584-0 www.schlecker.com |
| Annual Revenue: | $7.3 billion (2004) |
| Number of Locations: | 13,300 |
| Countries of Operation: | Germany, and 12 other European countries |
| Retail Classification: | Drugstore, hypermarket |

Schlecker is the largest drugstore retail chain in Europe, with more than 13,300 locations. Its strategy is "Drugstore Products for Europe," as evidenced by its recent expansion into Eastern Europe and Denmark. Its market share in its home nation, Germany, is over 70% — over 14 million Germans shop its stores each week.

Stores offer customers over 4,000 product lines in about 2,000 square feet of floor space, reflecting its origins as a discount operation. The chain began when the first store was opened by Anton Schlecker in 1975.

At present, familiar brand names predominate its shelves, but the company says these will be increasingly supplemented by Schlecker's own-brand products as the chain seeks to achieve 15% of sales from its own brands.

Stores are located in a range of locations — pedestrian zones, upscale streets and shopping centers, but also side streets, suburbs and residential areas. Customers find the same product lines in each country Schlecker serves: hair and body products, cleaning and washing items, baby food and baby care, hygiene products and tissues, and cosmetics and fragrances. The stores also offer some food items: coffees, sweets, soft drinks, wines and spirits, as well as tobacco and photography-related items.

Schlecker's prides itself on "permanently low prices" and special offers every week. Special offers are advertised through Schlecker's own magazine, the *Schlecker Revue*, with a print run of 1.5 million, through Schlecker-TV in Germany, and in weekly newspaper ads. Schlecker has been ranked by national media as one of the top five best places to shop in Germany.

*With more than 13,300 locations and over 4,000 products, Schlecker is the largest retail drugstore chain in Europe.*

*In addition to cosmetics, fragrances and baby care products, Schlecker offers food items, coffees, sweets, and wines and spirits.*

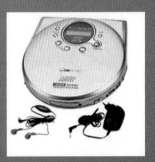

# The Seiyu, Ltd.

| | |
|---|---|
| **Parent Company/** **Corporate Name:** | **The Seiyu, Ltd.** |
| Corporate Retail Headquarters: | 1-1, Akabane 2-chome Kita-ku, Tokyo, Japan 115-0045 81-3-3598-7000 www.seiyu.co.jp |
| Annual Revenue: | $9.4 billion (2004) |
| Number of Locations: | 210 |
| Countries of Operation: | Japan, Hong Kong, Singapore, Vietnam |
| Retail Classification: | Supermarket, department store |

*S*eiyu offers its own private brands such as Food Delights and Seiyu Fine Select food products.

How do you say "Wal-Mart" in Japanese? Increasingly, the answer is The Seiyu, Ltd., which is adapting the expertise of the worldwide number-one retailer (which has a large stake in The Seiyu) to its supermarkets, department stores and shopping centers throughout Japan.

The Seiyu is integrating "the superior technologies and expertise of Wal-Mart," notably with its Smart System of unit management by product for sales and inventory, to enable instant access to daily sales volume figures. It is also working towards Wal-Mart's Every Day Low Price strategy.

The company is renovating many of its stores with an eye to Wal-Mart design in product displays and clear price markings. Simply Basic, Wal-Mart's global brand, and Kid Connection, a Wal-Mart private brand of toys, have been brought in.

Seiyu also offers its own private brands, Food Delights, West Win apparel, Seiyu Fine Select food products and Kankyo Yusen cosmetics.

Seiyu operates under a number of store brands. Seiyu, SSV and Sunny are its supermarkets. Livin is its department store. Some of its stores are anchors for its large shopping centers called, simply, The Mall.

*S*eiyu stores include Seiyu supermarkets and Livin department stores. The company's large shopping centers, called The Mall are anchored by some of its stores.

# The Sherwin-Williams Company

| | |
|---|---|
| **Parent Company/<br>Corporate Name:** | The Sherwin-Williams Company |
| Corporate Retail<br>Headquarters: | 101 Prospect West<br>Cleveland, OH 44115, United States<br>216-566-2000<br>www.sherwin-williams.com |
| Annual Revenue: | $4 billion (2004) |
| Number of Locations: | 2,643 |
| Countries of Operation: | The U.S., Canada, Mexico, Latin America |
| Retail Classification: | Specialty |

*Sherwin-Williams products include paints, finishes, coatings and varnishes sold under names such as Dutch Boy, Pratt & Lambert, Krylon and Minwax.*

Sherwin-Williams has been in business since 1866, manufacturing, distributing and selling coatings and related products.

Its product lines include Sherwin-Williams–labeled architectural coatings, industrial finishes and associated supplies through company-owned paint and wallcovering stores in all 50 states, Canada and several Latin American countries.

The company's product lines include Dutch Boy, Pratt & Lambert, Martin-Senour, Dupli-Color, Krylon, Thompson's and Minwax.

Sherwin-Williams also produces coatings for original equipment manufacturers in a number of industries and special-purpose coatings for the automotive aftermarket, industrial maintenance and traffic paint markets. Its automotive finishes and international coatings are available through company-operated branches and subsidiary distributors in the Americas, and elsewhere around the world.

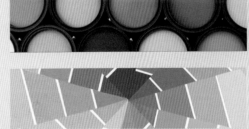

*T*he company also produces automotive coatings, equipment coatings and special purpose coatings for a number of industries.

Do You Have Everything For Your Painting Project?

# Shoprite Holdings

| | |
|---|---|
| **Parent Company/ Corporate Name:** | **Shoprite Group of Companies** |
| Corporate Retail Headquarters: | Corner William Dabs and Old Paarl Roads Brackenfell 7560, South Africa +27-21-980-4000 www.shoprite.co.za |
| Annual Revenue: | $4.9 billion (2004) |
| Number of Locations: | 786 |
| Countries of Operation: | South Africa, India and 15 other countries in Africa |
| Retail Classification: | Supermarket, hypermarket, convenience store |

*The Shoprite Group of companies began in 1979 with the purchase of a chain of eight Cape-based supermarkets and has grown to nearly 800.*

Africa's largest food retailer is The Shoprite Group of Companies, which operates 688 corporate outlets. Its customer base in South Africa includes some 10 million people, closely mirroring the demographic profile of the country. A trade study found that over 70% of South African households do their shopping at the group's stores.

Proudly South African, proudly African

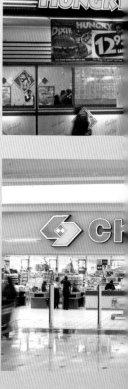

*Serving 10 million customers in South Africa, the Shoprite Group is Africa's largest food retailer.*

*The company operates Shoprite and Checkers supermarkets, Freshmark produce distribution centers and Hungry Lion fast food outlets.*

The chain operates under a number of brands and formats. There are 318 Shoprite supermarkets, 83 Checkers supermarkets, 19 Freshmark fresh produce distribution centers, 148 OK Furniture outlets, 19 Checkers Hypers, 48 Usave supermarkets, 23 House & Home stores and 50 Hungry Lion fast food outlets.

Store formats are geared to particular market segments. The Checkers supermarkets appeal to the mass middle market. Checkers Hyper and House & Home stores aim at the middle to upper end of the market. Shoprite and OK Furniture focus on the broad middle to lower market.

There is an OK Franchise division, through which Shoprite Group procures and distributes stock to 31 OK MiniMark convenience stores, 28 OK Foods supermarkets, 43 OK Grocer stores, five 8'Till Late outlets, 78 Megasave wholesale stores and 135 Sentra, Value stores and buying partners.

The Shoprite Group of Companies began in 1979 with the purchase of a chain of 8 Cape–based supermarkets. Various acquisitions and expansion strategies brought it to its market predominance of nearly 800 stores, including the 170-store Checkers chain in 1991. It entered the franchising field in 1995 when it acquired the central buying organization known as Sentra, which acted on behalf of 550 owner-manager supermarket members. It opened its first non–African store in India in 2004.

# SHV Holdings N.V.

| Parent Company/ Corporate Name: | SHV Holdings N.V. |
|---|---|
| Corporate Retail Headquarters: | Rijnkade 1<br>3511 LC Utrecht, The Netherlands<br>+31-30-2338833<br>www.shv.nl |
| Annual Revenue: | $4 billion (2004) |
| Number of Locations: | 140 |
| Countries of Operation: | Five in Asia, four in South America and Europe |
| Retail Classification: | Food |

*Makro is continually refining its management of perishables and non-food items and plans to increase both assortment and space for its perishables.*

# M

Makro is the retail division of SHV Holdings N.V., which also has interests in gas, capital equity, recycling, and exploration and production of oil and gas.

Makro is a cash-and-carry wholesaler with independent retailers and caterers as its most important customer groups. The company is an increasingly important part of the distribution process to the consumer, particularly to those to whom direct delivery is becoming less and less economically viable.

Its stores usually encompass between 60,000 and 80,000 square feet. The company is continually refining its management of both perishables and nonfood products, with plans to increase both the assortment and space for its perishables.

Makro South America is comprised of 81 stores, serving Argentina (13 stores), Brazil (43), Columbia (9) and Venezuela (17).

Makro Asia includes 59 stores, representing Thailand (23), Indonesia (13), Malaysia (8), Philippines (11) and China (4).

SHV opened the first Makro self-service wholesale store in Amsterdam in 1968, expanding in the next few years into other European countries. Throughout the 1970s and 1980s, SHV expanded its Makro business in South America and Asia. The company plans considerable expansion in northeast China.

*M*akro is a cash-and-carry wholesaler with independent retailers and caterers as its most important customer group.

# Skechers U.S.A., Inc.

| | |
|---|---|
| **Parent Company/ Corporate Name:** | **Skechers U.S.A., Inc.** |
| Corporate Retail Headquarters: | 228 Manhattan Beach Blvd Manhattan Beach, CA 90266 United States 310-318-3100 www.skx.com |
| Annual Revenue: | $920 million (2004) |
| Number of Locations: | 125 |
| Countries of Operation: | The US, Canada, the U.K., France, Germany and others |
| Retail Classification: | Footwear |

Skechers owns and operates 125 stores in the U.S., Canada and Europe. Their brands include Skechers Sport, Skechers Active, Skechers Work and Skechers Kids.

WE PUT THE S IN ACTION!

Skechers is a lifestyle-focused footwear store that designs, develops and markets a variety of footwear for trend-savvy people of all ages, although its target market is aged 12 to 24. (The phrase "skechers" is street slang for "gotta move.")

Founded in 1992, Skechers' products have grown from utility-style boots to include seven Skechers brands and five fashion lines for men and women. Brands include Skechers Sport, Skechers Active, Somethin' Else from Skechers, Skechers Work and Skechers Kids.

The separately branded series of fashion lines include Mark Nason (for men), 310 Motoring and Unltd. by Marc Ecko Footwear (both for men and boys), Red by Mark Ecko (women and girls), Michelle K Sport (women) and Michelle K Girl (girls).

In all, the company offers over 2,000 styles in products available in department and specialty stores in the U.S., Canada and Europe, and globally from Australia and Russia to Chile and India.

There are 125 company-owned and operated stores in the U.S., Canada and Europe. Thirty retail stores operate in key cities in 15 countries.

*S kechers develops and markets a line of trendy footwear for people of all ages, but is geared toward the 12-24 market.*

# Sonae SGPS SA

**Parent Company/**
**Corporate Name:**     **Sonae SGPS, SA**

Corporate Retail         Lugar do Espido via Norte, Apartado 1011
Headquarters:            Maia 4471-909, Portugal
                         +351-22-948-82-22
                         www.sonae.pt

Annual Revenue:          $9 billion (2004)

Number of Locations:     302

Countries of Operation:  Brazil, Portugal, Spain

Retail Classification:   Supermarkets, hypermarkets, convenience stores

*Sonae's retail subdivision, Modelo Continente runs over 400 hypermarkets and supermarkets under the names Modelo and Continente in Brazil and Portugal.*

Sonae was founded in 1959 as a wood products company in Maia, Portugal, specializing in high-pressure decorative laminates. During its rapid growth in the 1980s, it began diversifying through the acquisition of a supermarket chain, followed by the launch of its first hypermarket.

Its retail subdivision, Modelo Continente, runs over 400 hypermarkets, supermarkets and other stores in Portugal and Brazil. Its stores are known as the Modelo, Continente and Bonjour hypermarkets and convenience stores. Its stores in Portugal comprise one of the nation's largest supermarket chains.

Beyond the wood products and supermarket lines, Sonae also has interests in ownership, management and development of shopping centers in Portugal; fixed and mobile telecommunications; and tourism, construction, transport and risk capi-tal. Its shopping center division, responsible for the first regional mall in Portugal, focuses on building shopping centers adjacent to Sonae stores. Sonae is the largest private employer in Brazil.

*R*esponsible for the first regional mall in Portugal, Sonae focuses on building shopping centers adjacent to its stores.

# Staples

| | |
|---|---|
| **Parent Company/ Corporate Name:** | **Staples, Inc.** |
| Corporate Retail Headquarters: | 500 Staples Drive Framingham, MA 07102, United States 508-253-5000 www.staples.com |
| Annual Revenue: | $10.2 billion (2004) |
| Number of Locations: | 1,775 |
| Countries of Operation: | The U.S., Canada, Germany, The Netherlands, Portugal, the U.K. |
| Retail Classification: | Specialty |

*Staples stores are located in suburban malls and high-traffic urban areas. They offer low every day prices on more than 7,500 items.*

Staples launched the office supplies superstore industry with the opening of its first store in Brighton, Massachusetts, in 1986. It sought to provide small business owners with the same low prices on office supplies previously enjoyed only by large corporations.

Staples is now a multibillion retailer of office supplies, business services, furniture and technology to consumers and businesses in North America and Europe, with customers walking in, calling in or logging on.

*Staples sells office supplies, furniture, technology, and business services in over 1,700 locations in North America and Europe.*

The chain has nearly 1,600 stores operating in the U.S. and Canada, with over 175 stores in western Europe. Stores are typically located in suburban malls and high-traffic urban sites, and offer everyday low prices on over 7,500 supply items. A typical Staples superstore is about 20,000 square feet, but the company also operates smaller-format stores called Staples Express.

Stores offer a Copy & Print Center that provides on-site copying, printing and binding services. U.S. stores offer a Business Technology Center where customers can get computer upgrades, software installations and consultation by trained staff. U.S. superstores have build-to-order computer capacities and many business services such as payroll and Web services to its small business customers. All U.S. superstores have Internet Access Points and some superstores in densely populated cities operate 24 hours a day.

The company also has a business-to-business e-commerce program called StaplesLink.com, providing real-time inventory availability on products. The website (www.staples.com) serves small businesses. StaplesDirect is its catalog operation, offering low prices on 6,000 standard items and 25,000 items in its special-order catalog. Quill, acquired by Staples in 1998, is a direct marketing office supplies company.

*S*tores offer Copy and Print Centers that provide on-site copying, printing and binding services.

# Starbucks

| | |
|---|---|
| **Parent Company/<br>Corporate Name:** | **Starbucks Corporation** |
| Corporate Retail<br>Headquarters: | 2401 Utah Avenue South<br>Seattle, WA 98134, United States<br>206-447-1575<br>www.starbucks.com |
| Annual Revenue: | $6.4 billion (2005) |
| Number of Locations: | 7,600 |
| Countries of Operation: | The U.S. and 30 other countries |
| Retail Classification: | Food service |

*I*n 2001, the chain began to offer high-speed, wireless internet access.

*I*n addition to offering coffee, drinks, food items, coffee accessories, and CDs, Starbucks also offers a place to relax and socialize, at this Shanghai store.

It's no longer a cup of joe or java — it's often Starbucks when people want a quick cup of coffee on the road or while shopping.

Starbucks purchases and roasts high-quality whole bean coffees and sells them along with rich-brewed Italian espresso beverages, pastries, confections and coffee-related accessories and equipment in highly visible stores that are a gathering-point for the upscale consumer.

Beyond its retail stores, Starbucks sells whole bean coffees through a specialty sales group and supermarkets; bottled coffee drinks; a line of premium ice creams; and an assortment of premium teas.

The company's mission statement is to establish Starbucks "as the premier purveyor of the finest coffee in the world." It was founded in 1971 with its first store in Seattle's Pike Place market. Eleven years later it started offering coffee to fine restaurants and espresso bars. A company executive traveled to Italy in 1983, where he was impressed with the popularity of espresso bars in Milan, and brought the concept home. The total number of Starbucks locations grew from 17 in 1987 to 425 in 1994, 1,886 in 1998 and 7,659 in 2004.

The chain began to offer high-speed wireless internet access in its stores in 2001. The Starbucks Foundation has given many millions of dollars in grants to literacy programs, schools and community-based organizations across North America. It has established in-store relationships with Nordstrom, Barnes & Noble, the Albertson's supermarket chain and the Canadian bookstore chain Chapters Inc. Based on its popular in-house music program, Starbucks began selling CDs in 1995. It opened its 1000th Asia/Pacific store in Beijing in 2003.

# Takashimaya Company, Limited ⊛Takashimaya

**Parent Company/
Corporate Name:** Takashimaya Company, Limited

**Corporate Retail
Headquarters:** 5-1-5 Namba, Chuo-ku
Osaka, 542-8510, Japan
+81-6-6631-1101
www.takashimaya.co.jp

**Annual Revenue:** $8.5 billion (2004)

**Number of Locations:** 26

**Countries of Operation:** Japan and 7 other countries

**Retail Classification:** Department store

*T*akashimaya Company is the oldest department store chain in Japan. Their stores are found in Japan's largest cities, as well as in New York, Paris and London.

*T*

Takashimaya Company's 18 stores in Japan are the oldest department store chain in the country. It traces its history back to a cotton-goods store founded in Kyoto in 1831, and the modern company was established in 1919.

Its department stores are found in Japan's largest cities: Toyko, Osaka, Kyoto, Rakusai, Sakai, Wakayama and elsewhere. Its stores offer apparel, health and beauty items, housewares and jewelry. Overseas, the stores gravitate to each nation's largest city — New York, Paris and London, to mention a few. The company also has interests in restaurants, wholesaling, construction and real estate.

*T*akashimaya stores offer beauty and cosmetic products, apparel, jewelry and housewares.

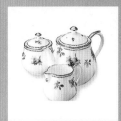

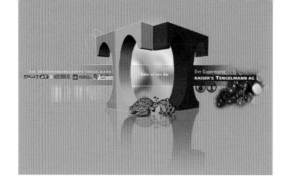

# Tengelmann Group

**Parent Company/
Corporate Name:**     **Tengelmann Warenhandelsgesellschaft KG**

Corporate Retail
Headquarters:     Wissollstrasse 5-43
45478 Mülheim an der Ruhr, Germany
+49-208-5806-7601
www.tengelmann.de

Annual Revenue:     $29 billion (2004)

Number of Locations:     1,700

Countries of Operation:     Germany, the U.S. Canada, China and 10 other European
countries

Retail Classification:     Supermarket, discount, specialty, drugstore

*A*mong Tengelmann's well-known brand names are the A & P supermarket chain in North America and Kaiser's Tengelmann supermarkets in Europe.

Founded in 1867, The Tengelmann Group is one of the world's largest retailers, operating about 7,200 stores throughout Europe, China and the U.S.

Among its well-known brand names are the North American supermarket chain A&P. In Europe, it operates the Kaiser's and Tengelmann supermarkets, kd drugstores, food discounter Plus, the OBI do-it-yourself store and the textile/food discounter KiK. Its supermarkets also operate as Dominion, Farmer Jack, Food Emporium, Super Foodmart and Waldbaums.

The company also operates the Interfruct cash-and-carry stores in Hungary and Slovakia, some apparel and liquor stores, and a number of smaller production houses such as the confectionery producers Wissol and Böem and meat-producing units. It has a number of food brands, including A&P Klasse Markenqualität, Birkenhof–controlled beef and Kaiser's Kaffee Klasse Aromaqualität. In the U.S. A&P stores, in-house brands include America's Choice, Master Choice, Health Pride and Savings Plus.

In Berlin and Munich, the company has been running a delivery service since 1997, allowing customers to place their orders via the Internet, fax or telephone.

*T*he Tengelmann Group is one of the world's largest retailers operating about 7,200 stores throughout the U.S. and Europe.

# Tesco

## TESCO
### *Every little helps*

| | |
|---|---|
| **Parent Company/ Corporate Name:** | **Tesco Plc** |
| Corporate Retail Headquarters: | Tesco House, Delamare Road, Hertfordshire Cheshunt EN8 9SL, United Kingdom +44-1992-632-222 www.tesco.com |
| Annual Revenue: | $62.5 billion (2004) |
| Number of Locations: | 2,100 |
| Countries of Operation: | The U.K. and 11 other countries in Europe and Asia |
| Retail Classification: | Supermarket, convenience store, hypermarket, department store |

*In response to consumer's lifestyle needs, Tesco continues to develop new products and services.*

# T

Tesco operates about 2,100 supermarkets and stores in other formats. The U.K. represents its biggest national commitment, with about 1,700 stores accounting for 80% of sales. Other European countries host about 265 stores contributing 11% of sales. Six Asian countries have a combined 187 stores, adding 8% of sales.

About half of Tesco's U.K. stores operate under the OneStop name, with another one-fourth known as Tesco Superstores. Its other brand names in the U.K. are Day & Nite stores, Tesco Express, Tesco Extra and Tesco Metro.

Tesco has a strong corporate responsibility to charitable causes. It is the U.K.'s biggest seller of Fairtrade products, whose sales benefit farmers and growers in developing countries. The company has also launched its Regeneration Partnership, wherein Tesco seeks to revitalize deprived communities and reclaim derelict sites through new Tesco stores.

The Tesco name represents the company's presence throughout much of the rest of the chain, except for 5 stores in Turkey known as Kipa and the 80-plus stores in Japan, operating as C&C Cash and Carry, Footlet, Kamechuru, Tsurukame and Tsurukame Land.

To respond to consumers' lifestyle needs, the company develops new products and services, such as the website (www.tesco.com) launched in 2001, Tesco Personal Finance (in 1996) and Tesco Telecoms (in 2003).

*The company's other U.K. brand names include Tesco Extra, Tesco Express and Tesco Metro.*

*Tesco operates about 2,100 supermarkets and stores in other formats. There are about 1,700 located in the U.K. and about 450 located in Europe and Asia.*

# Tiffany & Co.

| | |
|---|---|
| **Parent Company/ Corporate Name:** | Tiffany & Co. |
| **Corporate Retail Headquarters:** | 727 Fifth Avenue New York, NY 10022, United States 212-755-8000 www.tiffany.com |
| **Annual Revenue:** | $2.2 billion (2005) |
| **Number of Locations:** | 150 |
| **Countries of Operation:** | The U.S., Canada, Mexico, Brazil, Australia, and stores in many countries in Europe and Asia |
| **Retail Classification:** | Jewelry |

©Mark Milian

*Customers carry away their items wrapped in blue colored boxes. The color is known worldwide as Tiffany Blue.*

*Beyond its extensive selection of jewelry, Tiffany sells sterling silverware, china, crystal, stationery, fragrances and accessories.*

An international icon of stylish jewelry, Tiffany was established as Tiffany & Young in 1831 on Broadway in New York City. The company offered a revolutionary retailing idea — each item was marked with a nonnegotiable selling price. The first day's sales totaled $4.98. Soon thereafter, customers carried away their items in boxes colored the shade now known worldwide as Tiffany Blue. The first Tiffany catalog was published in 1845 and continues today.

*The company's specialty is fine jewelry, but it also puts its famous name on timepieces.*

In 1853, Charles Tiffany gained sole control of the company, shortened its name to his own, and made Tiffany synonymous with luxury. It was chosen to design a presidential pitcher for Lincoln's inaugural in 1861. Six years later, Tiffany became the first U.S. firm to win an award for the excellence of its silverware. Its sterling silver flatware, Audubon, was introduced in 1871 and remains the company's most popular pattern into the 21st century. Tiffany redesigned the Great Seal of the United States of America in 1885 and acquired some of the French Crown Jewels in 1887.

*Tiffany sells its goods exclusively through 150 Tiffany & Co. stores and boutiques throughout the world.*

Today, beyond its extensive selection of fine jewelry (82% of net sales in fiscal 2004), Tiffany sells timepieces, sterling silverware, china, crystal, stationery, fragrances and accessories. Tiffany's luster extended internationally with store openings in Japan in 1972 and London in 1986. Tiffany's 150 stores can now be found on five continents.

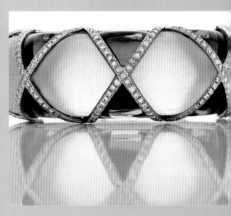

# TJX Companies, Inc.

**T·J·maxx**®

| | |
|---|---|
| **Parent Company/ Corporate Name:** | **TJX Companies, Inc.** |
| Corporate Retail Headquarters: | 770 Cochituate Road<br>Framingham, MA 01701, Uinted States<br>508-390-1000<br>www.tjx.com |
| Annual Revenue: | $15 billion (2005) |
| Countries of Operation: | The U.S., Canada, Ireland, the U.K. |
| Retail Classification: | Department store, specialty |

*T*JX Companies operates eight retail chains including T.J. Maxx in the U.S., T.K. Maxx in the U.K. and Winners in Canada.

*T.*J. Maxx, T.K. Maxx and Winners sell brand-name family apparel, accessories, women's shoes, housewares and jewelry at discount prices.

T

TJX Companies is comprised of eight businesses, most ubiquitous of which are the Maxx stores — T.J. Maxx in the U.S. and T.K. Maxx in Europe. The target customer for six of the eight businesses is the middle to upper-middle-income shopper who is conscious of value and fashion and fits the same profile as a department store shopper.

The first two T.J. Maxx stores opened in 1977 in Worcester and Auburn, Massachusetts. The chain expanded to include eight store brands:

- T. J. Maxx is the largest off-price apparel retailer in the U.S. Family apparel, women's footwear, accessories, jewelry and giftware are available at prices 20%–60% below regular department store and specialty store prices.

- Marshalls, acquired in 1995, is the second-largest off-price retailer in the U.S. It has brand-name family apparel, giftware, home fashions, footwear and accessories.

- T.K. Maxx, launched in 1994, is the British Isles' version of the main chain, offering off-price apparel and home fashions in the U.K. and Ireland.

- HomeSense introduced the home fashions off-price concept to Canada in 2001, offering a rapidly changing selection of cookware, linens, rugs, accent furniture and seasonal items.

- Winners, also in Canada, is patterned after T.J. Maxx, with off-price family apparel, giftware, fine jewelry, home fashions, accessories and women's footwear.

- HomeGoods is, a chain of off-price home fashion stores. Its home décor merchandise lines include furniture, giftware, rugs, bed and bath accessories, lamps and seasonal merchandise. Superstores called T.J. Maxx 'N More and Marshalls Mega-Stores couple HomeGoods with the superstore.

- Bob's Stores, acquired in 2003, varies somewhat from the typical TJX target customer by focusing on the apparel needs of men. It offers an extensive assortment of casual clothing, particularly activewear and workwear.

- A.J. Wright stores debuted in 1998, again varying somewhat from the shopper profile in that it reaches out to the moderate-income consumer. These stores offer value on brand-name family apparel and footwear, plus giftware and home fashions.

*HomeGoods in the U.S. and HomeSense in Canada are off-price home fashion stores. They offer furniture, rugs, giftware, accessories and seasonal items.*

# Toys "R" Us

| | |
|---|---|
| **Parent Company/ Corporate Name:** | **Toys "R" Us, Inc.** |
| Corporate Retail Headquarters: | 1 Geoffrey Way Wayne, NJ 07474-2030, United States 973-617-3500 |
| Annual Revenue: | $11.1 billion (2005) |
| Number of Locations: | 1,500 |
| Countries of Operation: | The U.S. and worldwide |
| Retail Classification: | Specialty |

*T*oys "R" Us operates about 700 stores in the U.S. and has expanded their concept to Canada, Europe and Japan.

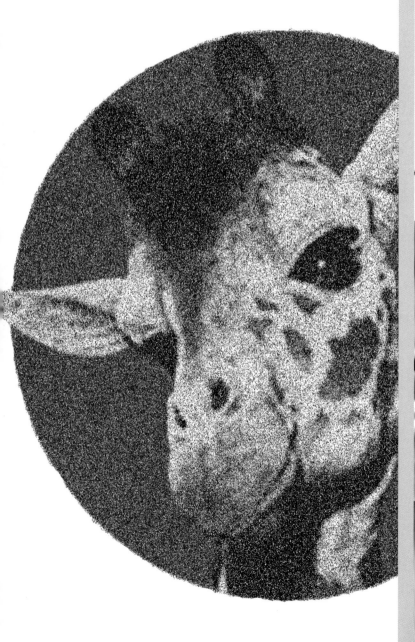

FOCUS ON THE FUTURE

W

With its familiar spokesanimal Geoffrey the giraffe, Toys "R" Us has grown from its emergence as a public company in 1978 to a worldwide presence of about 1,500 stores.

The company was founded by Charles Lazarus in 1948 as a baby furniture store in Washington, D.C. Responding to the need of postwar parents and grandparents for presents for the newly born baby boomers, Lazarus began selling toys at the store. His first toy supermarket opened in 1957, when his concepts of off-price and specialty retailing were revolutionary in the U.S.

The company's has four highly visible divisions:

- Toys "R" Us, one of the world's leading toy retailers, operates about 700 stores in the U.S. featuring specialized shops such as Animal Alley, Home Depot and "R" Zone.

- Toys "R" Us International has expanded the concept around the world, from Europe to Australia and from Canada to Japan.

- Kids "R" Us specializes in apparel for newborns through age 16. Back-to-school, active and dress-up fashions are available, along with accessories and shoes.

- Babies "R" Us The Baby Superstore is the largest baby product specialty store chain in the world. Debuting in 1996, the chain now has nearly 200 stores. It offers a baby registry and a wide range of juvenile products, including furniture, apparel, toys, strollers, car seats and infant care items.

*T*he company's divisions include Kids "R" Us specializing in apparel for children and Babies "R" Us, the Baby Superstore.

# Vendex KBB

VENDEXBB

| | |
|---|---|
| **Parent Company/ Corporate Name:** | **Vendex KBB B.V.** |
| Corporate Retail Headquarters: | De Klencke 6<br>1083 HH Amsterdam, The Netherlands<br>+31-205490500<br>www.vendexkbb.nl |
| Annual Revenue: | $5.5 billion (2004) |
| Number of Locations: | 1,700 |
| Countries of Operation: | The Netherlands and other European countries |
| Retail Classification: | Department, specialty |

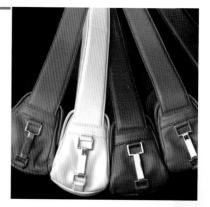

*V*endex KBB is a holding company for a diverse group of companies which includes department stores and specialty stores in seven European countries.

Vendex KBB is a holding company for a diverse group of operating companies in seven European countries. Its department stores include Vroom and Dreesmann.

Specialty stores include outlets for home furnishings, apparel and hard goods such as Hunkemoeller, Kreymborg, Kien, Claudia Straeter, Perry Sport, Stoutenbeek, Siebel, Dixons (not related to the British retailer), Wooncentrum, Lederland, Superdoe and Kijkshop.

About 85% of company sales come from within The Netherlands. It has also had operations in France, Denmark, Spain and Belgium. It has recently expanded its presence in the do-it-yourself industry, acquiring the Brico chain in Belgium and six Leroy Merlin stores.

*V*endex recently expanded into the do-it-yourself market when it acquired the Brico home improvement chain in Belgium.

*M*ost of the company's sales come from within The Netherlands. Their stores are also located in Denmark, France, Spain and Belgium.

# Wal-Mart Stores, Inc.

**WAL★MART**®

| | |
|---|---|
| **Parent Company/ Corporate Name:** | **Wal-Mart Stores, Inc.** |
| Corporate Retail Headquarters: | 702 Southwest Eighth Street Bentonville, AR 72716-0130, United States 501-273-4000 www.walmartstores.com |
| Annual Revenue: | $285 billion (2005) |
| Number of Locations: | 5,000 |
| Countries of Operation: | The U.S. and 12 other countries in the Americas, Europe and Asia |
| Retail Classification: | Discount, hypermarket, supermarket |

*It's a Big Deal!*

*I*n 1991, Wal-Mart went international with the opening of their membership-only warehouse store, Sam's Club, near Mexico City.

Store #1
Rogers, Arkansas
Then and Now

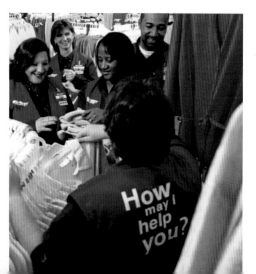

How may I help you?

*T*here are about 5,000 Wal-Mart stores and wholesale clubs across 10 countries. They operate on an "Every Day Low Price" philosophy.

Low Prices

*S*am Walton's "Three Basic Beliefs" still guide Wal-Mart stores today: respect for the individual, service to customers, and to strive for excellence.

Wal-Mart, the world's largest retailer, was created by the legendary Sam Walton. "Mr. Sam" established the "Three Basic Beliefs" that still guide his stores today; respect for the individual, service to customers, strive for excellence.

The self-service stores offer 36 departments' worth of general merchandise, including family apparel, health and beauty aids, household needs, electronics, toys, fabrics and crafts, lawn and garden, jewelry and shoes. Some stores offer a pharmacy, tire and lube express, garden center, snack bar or restaurant, optical center and/or one-hour photo service.

There are about 5,000 stores and wholesale clubs across 10 countries. There are several store formats. In addition to the Wal-Mart community stores, there are Supercenters that combine a full grocery line with general merchandise, under one roof. There are also Sam's Clubs, which are members-only warehouse clubs. There are also neighborhood markets and a website (www.walmart.com).

Wal-Mart went international in 1991, when a Sam's Club opened near Mexico City. Now, there are more than 1,300 units in Mexico, Canada, Brazil, Argentina, the U.K., Germany, China and Korea. The U.K. stores are known as Wal-Mart and ASDA. Wal-Mart acquired a minority interest in the Japanese retailer The Seiyu in 2002.

Wal-Mart is possibly the most-written-about retailer in the world, particularly for the quality of its customer service, inspired by "Mr. Sam." Among his credos is the "10-Foot Rule," which encouraged his associates to take with them: "Whenever you come within 10 feet of a customer, you will look him in the eye, greet him and ask him if you can help him."

# Yum! Brands, Inc.

| | |
|---|---|
| **Parent Company/ Corporate Name:** | Yum! Brands, Inc. |
| Corporate Retail Headquarters: | 1441 Gardiner Lane Louisville, KY 40213, United States 502-874-8300 www.yum.com |
| Annual Revenue: | $9.3 billion (2005) |
| Number of Locations: | 33,000 |
| Countries of Operation: | 100 |
| Retail Classification: | Food service |

*T*wo recent additions to the Yum! Brands family is Long John Silver's seafood chain and the A&W All American Food chain.

*T*he company is now offering multibrand restaurants, where more than one of its brands is sold at one site.

**M**ouths that water for fast food will know why this company is called Yum! Brands, Inc. It owns and operates the stores that offer some of the best-known brands of fast food in the world.

KFC (for Kentucky Fried Chicken) operates in 74 countries and territories around the world, featuring chicken flavored with 11 herbs and spices. Pizza Hut is in 84 countries, offering a variety of pizzas with different toppings, as well as pastas, salads, sandwiches, other food items and beverages. Taco Bell can be found in 17 countries and territories, specializing in Mexican style food products.

Two recent additions to the chain are Long John Silver's and A&W All American Food. Long John Silver's is America's largest quick-service seafood chain, with more than 1,200 units. A&W All American Food, famous for its root beer floats, serves hamburgers and other casual items.

In recent years, the company has begun offering multibrand restaurants, where one can purchase food products from two or more of the Yum! chains.

There are over 500 KFCs and 60 Pizza Huts in China alone. Korea boasts "the best Pizza Hut business in the world." The company is opening almost three new restaurants a day outside the U.S. Among the international locations, the (non–U.S.) stores in the Americas generate about 20% of company sales; Asia-Pacific about 32%; Greater China about 15% and Europe/South Africa about 25%

As a slogan for the multibrand company states, "Alone, we're delicious . . . together, we're Yum!"

*Y*um! Brands operates about 33,000 stores worldwide. There are over 500 KFCs and 60 Pizza Huts in China alone.